FASHIONING

AUTHORITY

The Development

FASHIONING

of Elizabethan

AUTHORITY

Novelistic Discourse

CONSTANCE C. RELIHAN

The Kent State University Press
KENT, OHIO, AND LONDON, ENGLAND

© 1994 by The Kent State University Press
Kent, Ohio 44242
ALL RIGHTS RESERVED
Library of Congress Catalog Card Number 93-32278
ISBN 0-87338-495-4
Manufactured in the United States of America

Library of Congress Cataloging-in-Publication Data
Relihan, Constance Caroline.
Fashioning authority : the development of Elizabethan novelistic discourse / Constance C. Relihan.
p. cm.
Includes bibliographical references and index.
ISBN 0-87338-495-4 ∞
1. English fiction—Early modern, 1500–1700—History and criticism. 2. Authority in literature. 3. Fiction—Technique. 4. Literary form. I. Title.
PR836.R45 1994
823'.309—dc20   93-32278
CIP

British Library Cataloging-in-Publication data are available.

for Tom

Lette this then suffice likewise for myne excuse, that my self seeyng trifles of no accoumpt, to be now best in season, and suche vanities more desired, then matters of better purpose, and the greatest parte of our writers, still busied with the like. So I haue put forthe this booke, because I would followe the fashion.

—Barnabe Riche, *Riche His Farewell to Militarie Profession*

Contents

Preface ix

Introduction
Elizabethan Contexts and Generic Anxiety 1

1 Prose, Poetry, and Popular Authority 17

2 Borrowed Authority
Appropriating "Italian Histories" 33

3 Constructing Voice, Subverting Narrative 55

4 Gender, Empowerment, and the Construction of Character 77

5 Authorizing Landscapes
The Power of Place 99

6 Constructing the Alien, Authorizing the Self 119

Conclusion
Novelistic Discourse and the Problem of Realism 140

Notes 144

Bibliography 162

Index 172

Preface

THE FOLLOWING study attempts to examine, both structurally and culturally, the role of Elizabethan prose fiction in the shifts in early modern literary culture that authorize the non-aristocratic reader's role in the reception of literature, the marketplace's role in the production and reception of prose texts, and the growth of prose as a medium for English narrative fiction. The mechanism for this investigation is the negotiation that occurs between the texts and six Others they establish for themselves—three primarily structural and three largely thematic and cultural. It has evolved slowly, and it has benefited from the enthusiasm and the skepticism it has engendered in those friends and colleagues who have read or heard portions of drafts privately and in conference settings. Shirley Nelson Garner, Lonnie Durham, the late Gordon W. O'Brien, and the members of University of Minnesota Department of English, who nurtured the development of an earlier version of this manuscript, have been invaluable supporters. It has also been strengthened by the additional readings of Arthur F. Kinney, Thomas P. Roche, Jr., John Wall, and the Kent State University Press's anonymous reader: I can only hope that I have made good use of their insights. My colleagues at Auburn University have stoically seen me through the process of revision, and I am particularly grateful to Dennis Rygiel for his support. My greatest debt, both intellectual and personal, is to Thomas M. O'Shea. Without his thoughtful criticism, wit, and unfailing confidence in my abilities, this book would never have been written.

I have not altered the spellings of the early modern texts cited, although I have expanded contractions and replaced the long *s*. Because there seems to be no scholarly consensus on how to spell the name of the primary author I discuss, I have chosen the spelling that appears on the title page of his *Farewell to Militarie Profession:* Barnabe Riche. References in the text to "Barnaby Rich" and "Barnaby Riche" are the result of this academic confusion. The titles of the individual narratives of Riche's *Farewell* have been slightly condensed.

An earlier draft of a portion of chapter 4 was published in *Cahiers Élisabéthains* 37 (1990): 9–15. I wish to thank the editors for permitting its appearance here.

FASHIONING

AUTHORITY

Introduction

Elizabethan Contexts & Generic Anxiety

THIS INVESTIGATION into Elizabethan novelistic discourse arises from two sets of concerns: those surrounding the culture that produced and was produced by these texts and those arising from the nature of these works as narrative literature. How do prose fictions by such writers as Deloney, Sidney, Lyly, Nashe, and Riche address the conditions in which they were written, their writers, and their readers? While these texts are engaged in producing a cultural environment conducive to their reception, they are also producing new modes of literary narrative, participating in the gradual transformation of narrative from a spoken, communal activity to a personal, silent encounter between an individual and a book—participating, too, in the generic shift from verse to prose as the dominant mode of narrative presentation.

These two rather divergent perspectives (the first historical, the second generic) combine in this study to form an analysis that is simultaneously concerned with the synchronic and the diachronic dimensions of the texts. It probes the means by which writers of a form lacking a strong generic tradition or a well-established readership were able to manipulate narrative structures and cultural concerns in order to define themselves and their readers within Elizabethan culture. In the process of defining modes of novelistic discourse, Elizabethan writers were able to derive a sense of subjectivity for themselves and their readers.

I have not tried to isolate for investigation a single category of fictional prose. Romances (Sidney's *Arcadia,* Lodge's *Rosalynde* and *A Margarite of America*), novels or proto-novels (Deloney's *Jack of Newbury* and *The Gentle Craft*), court fiction (Lyly's *Euphues* and Gascoigne's *Master F.J.*), translated novellas (Painter's *Palace of Pleasure*), criminal pamphlets (Greene's cony-catching texts and Harmon's *A Caveat for Common Cursitors*), and the picaresque (Nashe's *The Unfortunate Traveller*) all provide evidence to support claims about the fiction as a whole. In addition to these works, the greatest emphasis will be devoted to Barnabe Riche's *Farewell to Militarie Profession,* a collection of translated and original narratives bound together by a very prominent narrative voice. These disparate texts have been grouped together because they all share a common origin in the upheavals in English culture that produced an explosion of prose fiction during the later half of the sixteenth century. Changes in educational opportunities, socioeconomic structures, access to European literature, and literacy rates combine to create an environment more hospitable to prose fiction than had been previously present in England. Paul Salzman sees increased literacy as a key influence on the flourishing of Elizabethan prose narrative:

> The sudden proliferation of modes of fiction at this time reflects the increase in literacy during the last quarter of the sixteenth century. E. H. Miller estimates 50 percent literacy by 1600, and H. S. Bennett provides interesting figures which link this with a sudden increase in the production of fiction in the second half of the sixteenth century: the period 1558–1603 produced three times the amount of fiction found from 1475 to 1558.[1]

While Miller's literacy figures need to be viewed critically, and while we need to be cautious about relying too heavily on literacy alone as a central cause of generic change,[2] Salzman's conclusions suggest the reason for the scope and nature of this study: distinctions among modes of fictional prose are of less concern than are the cultural conditions that authorized the production of such a large number of diverse fictions during Elizabeth I's reign.

My goal is not to locate the first modern novel in the sixteenth century (although a case has been recently made that that distinction should be awarded to William Baldwin's *Beware the Cat*[3]) or to trace those elements within it that much twentieth-century criticism of fiction identifies as merging to produce the "realism" of the eighteenth-century novel. Rather, my goal is to place Elizabethan fictional prose within the larger history of novelistic discourse, which neither began with the development of "formal realism" nor lamented the so-called "death of the novel." Within this broader scope, the subcategories become less significant to the movement of fiction as a whole. Instead, what becomes foregrounded are ways in which the fictions attempt to authorize and define their own—and their readers'—desires and concerns.

Obviously, such an approach to generic concerns risks diminishing the historical and cultural process in which these texts were engaged. In "The Life and Death of Literary Forms," Alastair Fowler has observed just this difficulty. "All genres," he comments, are "mutable" and derive their meaning from a specific frame of reference, and this is certainly true, within a narrow sense. "Fiction" means something to a late-twentieth-century reader of English literature that it could not have meant to someone unable to read the narrative experiments of, say, James Joyce. And it is a term that is, technically, an anachronism when applied to the non-factual prose narratives of the Elizabethan period. As Lennard J. Davis and Michael McKeon have demonstrated, "fiction" is not a term its early practitioners or their readers used. Instead they termed their work "pamphlets," "histories," "romances," or, as in Sidney's *Defence*, "poetry." Nonetheless, "fiction" is the current category into which their work falls, and it is as fiction that we read it. The difficulties seventeenth-century booksellers had categorizing these texts do not prohibit our placing them within a history of fiction, a history perhaps most succinctly described in Bakhtin's analysis of the novel's modes of stylistic development in his "Discourse on the Novel."[4]

Bakhtin's analysis depends not so much on the length, subject matter, or descriptive "realism" of fiction as it does on the nature of the discourse that is essential for novelistic writing. Novelistic discourse requires "the destruction of any absolute bonding of ideological meaning to language," the destruction of "mythological thinking"—the kind of thinking the early Lukács identified with the epic. Once language is freed from this "absolute bonding" to ideology, and is, in Bakhtin's terms, "no longer conceived as a sacrosanct and solitary embodiment of meaning and truth, [it] becomes merely one of the many possible ways to hypothesize meaning." The split of language from ideology creates a decentering of "literary and language consciousness . . . [which] will occur only when a national culture loses its sealed-off and self-sufficient character, when it becomes conscious of itself as only one among *other* cultures and languages."[5] Such decentered language embodies the language of competing ideologies and cultures: it exhibits "heteroglossia," and it is the presence of heteroglossia which defines novelistic discourse within Bakhtin's analysis.

For Bakhtin, the length of the prose work becomes less crucial than the nature of the discourse within it. Such a minor point is significant in light of my grouping of Painter's *Palace of Pleasure* and Riche's *Farewell to Militarie Profession,* texts that compile short narratives, within the category of novelistic discourse. The Elizabethan anthologies I discuss portray the uncertainties of artistic authority and cultural meaning that the longer examples of novelistic discourse also delineate. In fact, the more numerous locations in which a narrative voice can intrude into these collections help to strengthen the reader's sense of the texts' conflicting ideologies and perspectives.

It is the relation, then, of these texts to the conflicting ideological contexts of Elizabethan culture that I intend to foreground. Simultaneously, the focus on novelistic discourse as a category, a category that the writers themselves did not recognize, is intended to assert the usefulness of a synchronic grouping of Elizabethan novelistic discourse with later texts in that tradition: such a grouping should strengthen our understanding of the nature of English fiction even as it broadens our sense of Elizabethan culture.

What the following study will produce is an interpretation of fictional prose texts that operated on the margins of late-sixteenth-century English literary culture, focusing on the ways in which the period's novelistic discourse positioned itself as Other in relation to cultural and literary ideological authority. The individual chapters analyze six different ways in which Elizabethan novelistic discourse isolated narrative and thematic concerns as a way of establishing its own artistic authority and the sense of authority of its readers. These six different approaches contribute to both my historical and generic goals. The first three chapters foreground narrative concerns: the uses of poetry to derive artistic authority, the relation of translated novellas to the development of prose texts, and the narrative strategies employed to create the particular sense of subjectivity found within the discourse. While these chapters stress narrative technique, they also situate the fiction within Elizabethan culture. They demonstrate the ways in which writers' use of and discomfort with specific narrative techniques become means by which the writers legitimate their art form and the act of reading their texts. The second half of this study addresses "thematic" concerns that expose the ways in which Elizabethan novelistic discourse dramatizes ideological conflicts within the individual texts, their writers, and their readers. These chapters focus on the texts' relation to cultural instead of narrative Others: women, the sense of place, and Eastern cultures. By analyzing the interaction of these texts with Others that consciously challenge prevailing ideologies, it is possible to view more distinctly the ways in which the period's novelistic discourse addressed ideological conflicts not only within sixteenth-century literary culture but within Elizabethan culture as a whole.

I

The decision to take as the central text for this analysis Barnabe Riche's *Farewell to Militarie Profession* (1581) is based on two factors. First, my concern with highlighting the role novelistic discourse played in Eliabethan culture is aptly mirrored by Riche's interest in defining modes of presentation and action for his texts and his readers. *Riche His Farewell to Militarie Profession* (as it is formally titled) presents what can be seen as the encapsulation of many of the prominent movements, themes, and techniques of novelistic discourse within late-sixteenth-century England. It consists of eight short stories (three of which are loose translations from Giraldi Cinthio's *Hecatommithi*) framed by prefaces and a conclusion that present a strong narrative voice, a voice that is present in less overt ways during the work as a whole. The stories themselves are of several types: "Sappho Duke of Mantona," for instance, is a lengthy tale about the problems of a soldier during a time of peace; "Twoo Brethren" describes the rollicking affairs of the independent wife of a gentleman's son; "Fineo and Fiamma" presents a tale of adventure reminiscent of Heliodoran romance. Regardless of the fictional mode of the individual tales, varieties of romantic love, its obstructions and its strength, figure prominently within these novellas and become central to the conflicting values and systems of social relations that the *Farewell* as a whole explores.[6] Because of its diversity, Riche's text constitutes an appropriate document around which to center discussion on the kinds of authority Elizabethan novelistic discourse encourages. While not preventing the inclusion of other writers in my argument, such a strategy will allow me to draw the fullest examples from Riche and discuss in less detail other narrative works that function in a similar manner.

The choice of Riche's *Farewell* as the central text is also in part idiosyncratic: I feel some temptation to justify my choice with an echo of David Margolies's general defense of his interest in Elizabethan fiction and claim that I have selected Riche's text "because I like it."[7] But there are more compelling reasons for preferring it to a more nearly canonical text like *Euphues* or *Jack of Newbury*. Aside from the variety of issues and narrative approaches the *Farewell* contains, it is also a significant work because of the character of the author and his uncertain relation to the classes and modes of power about which he writes.

The brief biography by T. M. Cranfill and Dorothy Bruce presents Barnabe Riche as a man uncertain of his position in society. Like the narrator of the *Farewell*, Riche felt himself to be a career soldier within a society that no longer appreciated dedication to the military life. He seems to have felt out of place in a society that stressed the qualities of the courtier more than those of a soldier (although I imagine the Irish subjected to English control would have questioned Riche's analysis of his culture's values). His mental anxiety is accompanied by material anxiety: Riche appears to have become progressively unstable financially during Elizabeth I's reign although he maintained a position as a captain in her (and, later, King James's) army. He spent several years serving in Ireland (where the *Farewell* was written), but he was often out of sympathy with those controlling Dublin and was the victim of harassment and violence. He spent much of his time in courtrooms; and, after his return to England, he seems to have relied heavily upon an annuity from the crown and upon what he could earn from his writing (he published approximately twenty-six texts on a variety of subjects, although John Leon Lievsay has raised questions about the originality of Riche's work). Two of his other texts, *The Aduentures of Brusanus, Prince of Hungarie* and *The Straunge and Wonderfull Aduentures of Don Simonides*, also belong to the tradition of novelistic discourse. The generic variety of the *Farewell* combines with Riche's marginal position to present a means of viewing the complexities of Elizabethan novelistic discourse. Because of Riche's insecurities on both formal and personal levels, the texts of the *Farewell* reveal the codes, both cultural and structural, that fiction tries to "conjure away," to use Roland Barthes's phrase.[8]

In all fairness, however, I should admit that previous studies do not seem to see in Riche the varied and fascinating substance and style I see. Lievsay's "A Word about Barnaby Rich," published in 1955, is the most damning. Considering the whole of Riche's career and not the *Farewell* in particular, Lievsay argues that Riche is primarily a plagiarist who makes "hash of a borrowed passage." In a comment typical of his essay's tone, Lievsay asserts of Riche's *Honestie of This Age* (1614) that its "disjointed, lame, and utterly unoriginal performance makes no memorable contribution either to letters or morals." Much specific criticism of Riche considers his narratives primarily in their function as dramatic sources, as Margaret Schlauch has shown, but some attention has been paid to the specifics of his text as well. Suzanne Hull has noted that the *Farewell* is one of the few Elizabethan texts that claims female readers as a primary audience. Anticipating Hull to a certain degree, Schlauch cites as one of Riche's primary strengths his ability to adopt a "chatty" and intimate tone toward his reader, a comment which may imply an audience that is at least partly female. Schlauch further comments that several of Riche's techniques for achieving intimacy with the reader come from the jestbook tradition, a fact that she says "indicates a certain approximation between popular and sophisticated literature." Thematically, Schlauch stresses Riche's ability to create a sense of realism by stressing human nature as a motivating factor, creating "homey English environments," and occasionally emphasizing economic motives.[9]

More recent historians of Elizabethan novelistic discourse do not share Schlauch's favorable response to the *Farewell*, however, and Riche has consequently received less thorough treatment in other general histories of the period's fiction. Walter R. Davis, whose *Idea and Act in Elizabethan Fiction* remains a very influential study of these texts, find much less emphasis on human action in the unraveling of Riche's plots. In reference to "Sappho Duke of Mantona," Davis states that the plot depends not on "who you are and what you want, but only . . . where you are and what means will be used by fortune to get you somewhere else." Whereas Schlauch's reading of Riche emphasizes the hominess of Riche's settings, Davis stresses the vastness of space in the *Farewell* and its lack of specificity. Davis's reservations about Riche, and those of literary historians who devote less time to him, seem to stem from an emphasis on locating the narratives either in relation to the novel in the form described in Ian Watt's *The Rise of the Novel* or in relation to cultural factors and rhetorical traditions as opposed to generic considerations.[10] Linking both approaches to Elizabethan novelistic discourse illuminates both the competing cultural forces within the early modern period and the history of prose fiction in English.

II

The cultural forces on which this study dwells are those that combine to address issues of authority for both the writers of Elizabethan novelistic discourse and their readers. As Jacqueline Miller has suggested, the issue of authority in sixteenth-century English literature was a problem in transition. The culture placed strong emphasis upon classical texts as models for literary forms and subjects. The influx of these texts, as well as European works, prompted debate over the nature of literary art, its function within society, and the characteristics of its audience.[11] As the following chapter will suggest, one significant area of contention was the forms literary poetry, or "poesy," to use Sidney's all-inclusive term, should adopt.

The position of novelistic discourse in the debate on the nature of poetry is difficult to identify precisely because few contemporary critics and theorists bothered to do just that. In *A Defence of Poetry*, Sidney terms Boccaccio a poet and says that "there have been many most excellent poets that never versified" (27), such as Heliodorus. Sidney's statement that "it is feigning notable images of virtues, vices, or what else, with that delightful teaching, which must be the right describing note to know a poet by" (27) is perhaps the clearest statement on the relationship of prose to verse. Yet, regardless of the ease with which modern critics accept Sidney's perspective, the degree to which his view was accepted during the period must be questioned. Although Bacon argues that a "fained history" may be written equally well "in Prose as in Verse," and Puttenham acknowledges that prose histories that are "fained and vntrue" are worthy of interest if they are constructed "for example and good information of the posteritie," nonetheless Puttenham's *Arte of Englishe Poesie* does not dwell at any length on the techniques of prose, except in the sense that rhetorical figures are as apt for prose as for verse.[12]

Other contemporary theorists seem less willing to make the equation between poetry and artful prose that Sidney and Puttenham express. For instance, in "Certayne Notes of Instruction" Gascoigne draws a clear line between what techniques are suitable for poetry and prose: although the same rhetorical figures may be used in both, "they serue more aptly and haue greater grace [in poetry] than they haue in prose." The equation made between poetry and verse becomes clearer if one examines William Webbe's *A Discourse of English Poetrie* (1586), in which definitions of poetry become tied to discussions of meter, and Sir John Harington's *A Brief Apology for Poetry* (1591), which defines poetry as comprised of "invention" (or fiction) *and* verse combined. The crucial distinction Thomas Nashe and Gabriel Harvey make, however, is between poetry and pamphlets. Harvey never calls a writer of prose a poet unless he is referring to Sidney. Nashe, in his preface to *Menaphon,* clearly establishes that poet and pamphleteer are two distinct categories; yet he does not feel that a preface to a prose romance is an inappropriate place to discuss the nature of English poetry and verse forms.[13]

I summarize this strain in Elizabethan critical thought to try to create a place for the early writer of novelistic discourse. His or her status, artistically speaking, was ambiguous. There was still debate about whether English poetry should use classical metrical patterns, and discussion about the artistic merit of prose was brief. Even the term Nashe and others use, "pamphleteer," masks any claim—artistic or otherwise—for the writer beyond the economic exigencies of the bookstall. How, then, is novelistic discourse to gain a readership, become distinct from news pamphlets, and gain credibility and an alignment with art?

Authority for Elizabethan fiction writers is certainly not only dependent upon or related to their use of prose. It is connected to their exteriority to the literary system of the period, a system that tended to view literary production as primarily metrical. In addition, many writers of prose fictions, such as Riche, Deloney, and Lodge, wrote for neither of the two clearly defined audiences: the stage or the courtly/aristocratic audience. A few writers, such as Sidney and Gascoigne, were generally in a more secure cultural position, yet their involvement in the production of devalued prose fictions helped to keep them, as Richard Helgerson has persuasively argued in *The Elizabethan Prodigals,* temporarily exterior to the Elizabethan literary system.[14]

The line Riche and other pamphleteers trod between art and the marketplace was fine, and it was made even finer by their choice of audience. Laura Caroline Stevenson's *Praise and Paradox: Merchants and Craftsmen in Elizabethan Popular Literature* suggests that the groups identified in her title were readers of pamphlets as well as their occasional subject. In addition, Louis B. Wright's classic study of the Elizabethan "middle class," regardless of any reservations we may have about its assumptions concerning sixteenth-century social hierarchies, is still valuable for documenting the number of publications on various subjects aimed at shopkeepers and guildsmen, and their wives, mothers, and sisters. Lawrence Stone, often drawing on Wright, has also noted the range of publications in Elizabethan England and has recognized the popularity of lurid accounts of crimes. Such observations suggest that there was a strong pull away from the courtly audience poetry usually addressed.[15] Appeals to these readers, who comprised not the influential and monied audience literature usually addressed, seem to cause a level of anxiety in the authors that becomes intolerable. Faced with uncertainty about the legitimacy or authority of the form in which they wrote, their status as "pamphleteers," and the untraditional nature of the audience they addressed, these writers tried to define their own cultural identity and that of their readers through the use of narrative structures as well as subject matter.

The economic position of these writers and their audience is crucial. Lawrence Stone and others have demonstrated that the Elizabethan period was one of tremendous economic and social change.[16] More peers were being created, and more peers were losing money. Marriages into the gentry were becoming an important source of economic salvation for the aristocracy; more merchants and tradesmen were establishing themselves in London; and there was less dependence upon the traditional landlord-tenant bond. In addition, greater dependence upon the Queen for military protection and economic advancement was developing.

The importance of these changes for writers of novelistic discourse cannot be overlooked. Margolies's *Novel and Society in Elizabethan England* summarizes very well the educated writer's position during the upheavals of the late sixteenth century. He points to the decreasing patronage caused by the erosion of feudal tradition and the centralization of the aristocracy at court as primary difficulties for the Elizabethan writer. Furthermore, he cites the increased enrollment of members of the artistocracy in universities as augmenting contention with educated non-aristrocratic humanists for the few court positions available. These non-aristocrats, displaced by their aristocratic fellow graduates, turned to writing, "which seemed a natural outlet for educated men denied public service." As Margolies illustrates, these writers could find an audience of university-educated gentry who aspired to court preferment and members of the growing merchant and trade classes who "had cultural needs which could not be served adequately by literature for the Court or traditional oral culture. They needed something that recognised their lack of accommodation in the inherited feudal ideology, that reflected the concerns of their own lives and embodied their own attitudes."[17] The educated writers, however, were ambiguously placed in relation to this audience because they still held in abeyance a desire for court preferment or aristocratic patronage. As Margolies suggests, to enter the marketplace of the bookstall was an ungentlemanly act; it violated the norms of the very class to which the writers aspired even as it provided their only means of entrance into that class.

The audience Margolies describes remains a shadowy group. Louis B. Wright's discussion of grammar and dame schools in the period suggests a fair number of readers, and Margaret Spufford's *Small Books and Pleasant Histories* addresses the issue of readership more directly. Although her focus is on seventeenth-century pamphlets and chapbooks, she does make interesting suggestions about the readership of Elizabethan works. She bases much of her discussion on the percentage of men able to sign their name. Such a method is somewhat inaccurate, she recognizes, because reading and writing were not taught simultaneously. Within the non-aristocratic classes, boys were first taught to read—probably by the age of seven—and were taught to write later, if they were not pulled from school by their parents for economic reasons (that is, if their families could not manage without their money-earning potential in the family fields or business). Female children were not always taught to write. Acknowledging the limitations of writing ability as an indicator of reading skills, Spufford uses statistics on name-signing ability to derive an absolute minimum reading public of 20 percent of adult men in 1642, and, citing research by David Cressy, a 15-percent figure for laborers who could write between 1580 and 1700. Since these percentages are for those able to write instead of read, we can assume higher figures; and the literacy rate for London residents can also be assumed to be higher, since Londoners had greater access to books and schools. The case for the existence of a broader reading public is further advanced by the number of works, such as those by Deloney, that have craftsmen or tradesmen as subjects. Such a conclusion is also supported by the number of works intended for servants or apprentices, and by the desire Spufford sees in many works to appeal to a wide range "of the urban and rural lower sections of society, from merchants and apprentices in towns, and from country farmers to day labourers in the countryside." Nonetheless, it is difficult to accept the 50 percent literacy rate Salzman cites, and the restrictions on the loose educational system Christopher Hill describes further problematize such an optimistic assessment of sixteenth-century readership.[18]

The wide range of kinds of readers and their increased numbers support the assumption that varying kinds of texts were constructed to satisfy different social and economic groups. Novelistic discourse, with its non-artistic nature and frequently non-aristocratic subjects and characters, seems designed to appeal to those segments of the reading public who could easily identify with the problems of a struggling apprentice (such as we see during the first section of *Jack of Newbury*) or the plight of a destitute girl (as in Nicholas Breton's *The Miseries of Mavillia*). This non-aristocratic primary audience gained access to literacy since education became much more widely available during the period. The second half of the sixteenth century saw the establishment of more schools of various kinds—not just schools that would prepare sons of the wealthy for the universities, but petty schools, grammar schools, and dame schools as well, in which the sons and daughters of guild members, merchants, and laborers in London and other sizable cities were taught to read.[19]

Furthermore, Suzanne Hull has concluded that although men wrote most of the period's books for a male audience, the number of works containing direct appeals to female readers or dedications to specific women suggest the presence of a considerable female readership. General support for Hull's assessment can be found as early as Louis B. Wright's "The Reading of Renaissance English Women," which discusses female attendance at petty schools and educational treatises such as Richard Mulcaster's *Positions Wherein Those Primitive Circumstances Be Examined, Which Are Necessarie For the Training up of Children* (1561), which, Wright notes, "suggests women were sufficiently educated to read English works." Margaret Spufford also cites the existence of women who taught reading and the presence of female children in rudimentary schools which taught reading, sewing, knitting, and spinning, as indicators of women readers. Dale Spender, on the other hand, draws on Antonia Fraser's *The Weaker Vessel* to conclude that seventeenth-century girls had little chance of being taught to read, and she claims that women were not "an audience for women's books."[20] This conclusion, it would seem, is hard to support. Of course, economics is key here: wealthy girls were much more likely to receive some education than were the poor. Nonetheless, it seems likely that a group of female readers did exist.

The period's novelistic discourse also supports the contention that women could read: Riche's heroine in "Twoo Brethren" reads a lawyer's letter, Deloney's Margaret in *Thomas of Reading* reads a maid's love letter (although she does so to the astonishment of the other maids),[21] and Nicholas Breton's title character in *The Miseries of Mavillia* is taught to read by her laundress stepmother who ignores the girl's complaints about the agony of studying. We must conclude that a female reading public did exist, a reading public that complemented the female auditors who had been typically imagined as part of the general audience for narrative texts such as Boccaccio's *Decameron,* Chaucer's *Canterbury Tales,* and Spenser's *Faerie Queene* or as a primary constituent of the writer's intended audience, as is the case with Sidney's *Old Arcadia,* Lodge's *A Margarite of America,* and Lyly's *Euphues and his England.* These facts do not deny the presence of courtly readers for works of Elizabethan novelistic discourse (the frequent prefaces and dedications to aristocratic figures suggest at least the hope that these works would lead to preferment), but they suggest that the court audience was often secondary, an audience that could identify with and enjoy these texts through a form of displacement rather than through a sense of immediate identification.

III

Shifts toward an audience newly come to see itself capable of intellectual and socioeconomic advancement produce changes in modes of literary production. Simultaneously, access to the bookstall and to a new class of readers alters the structures and subjects writers employ. The period's shifting grounds of cultural contention have been observed in various forms, one suggestive example being Frank Whigham's discussion of the role courtesy literature played in the transformations that created early modern English culture. Like Castiglione's *The Courtier,* Ascham's *The Scholemaster,* and Vives's *Education of a Christian Woman,* works Whigham calls manuals that provide the "'inside dope' for threading through the mazes of power," Elizabethan novelistic discourse similarly— if less overtly—provided its readers with guidance on negotiating the boundaries that established socioeconomic difference. Although less expressly didactic than courtesy literature, works like Nashe's *The Unfortunate Traveller,* Riche's *Farewell,* and Sidney's *Arcadia* similarly investigate and critique notions of social hierarchy. Through the creation and probing of a variety of what may be called "threatening Others," to use Stephen Greenblatt's term, Elizabethan novelistic discourse negotiates the cultural place of its newly literate readers and its generically marginal authors, creating literary comfort in narrative prose for those who failed to find it in poetry.[22]

1

Prose, Poetry, and Popular Authority

—

THE DIFFICULTY for the writer of Elizabethan novelistic discourse, as Renaissance poetic theory demonstrates, is the lack of literary, fictional models in prose. As William Nelson observes:

> Poets and dramatists had a great classical body of fiction for precedent; those who wrote stories in prose did not. The notable examples of classical prose are historical, philosophic, rhetorical, or didactic; ancient prose fiction familiar to Renaissance writers is represented by only a scattering of very various works, none of them of the stature of the *Aeneid* and most subject to the accusation of frivolity.[1]

While the medieval period provided English storytellers with some native prose models, most notably Malory's *Le Morte Darthur*, that supplemented the dearth classical culture provided, fiction writers of the Elizabethan period still operated from a disadvantage: their genre was generally viewed as non-literary; they were not artists, but writers for the marketplace.

One response to the absence of literary authority created by the arguments of courtesy literature and Renaissance literary theory was to embed within artistically marginalized prose the irrefutable art form, verse. Drawing from Continental sources, such as Sannazaro's *Arcadia* (1504)[2] and *The Diana* of Montemayor

(1559), writers as diverse in style as Sidney, Deloney, and Nashe found reasons to include poetic texts—either as found objects or as means of plot advancement—into their prose. This strategy finds its most developed presentation in Gascoigne's *The Adventures of Master F.J.*, but it is also employed in two of Riche's novellas ("Sappho Duke of Mantona" and "Nicander and Lucilla"), Deloney's *Jack of Newbury* (1594), and Lodge's *A Margarite of America* (1596), to name just a few of the works that attempt to achieve authority in this fashion. What is important about this list is that it illustrates the ways in which what was originally a romance convention spreads from its expected location in works such as Sidney's *Arcadia* to novella collections and "bourgeois" fiction as well.

These varieties of fiction provided the often non-aristocratic audience of Elizabethan novelistic discourse a means of imagining themselves in a new way through the inclusion of poetry within prose. Poetry within the texts allowed them to experience at least transitory connections to a recognizable literary form; moreover, it enabled the non-aristocratic audience to see itself engaged in an artistic process. As poetry transformed temporarily the pamphlets into traditional literary art, the readers became momentarily aristocratic during the process of reading. Once questions about the authority of novelistic discourse had been deferred, it was possible for the pamphleteers to define themselves and their readers thematically. Thomas Lodge's *A Margarite of America* (1596) provides a clear example of how poetry can function within fictional prose to establish a sense of the pamphlets as works of literary art and of their readers as members of an educated group able to recognize and interpret literature.[3]

Margarite, which may be broadly termed a romance, narrates the adventures of an evil prince and the unfortunate princess who loves him. Interspersed throughout the prose text are several poems that either describe characters' emotions or are presented as found objects (such as the poem—carved into a bedframe—that describes murals in a castle bed chamber). Toward the work's conclusion, however, the narrator presents his readers with a series of love poems that the evil prince, Arsadachus, wrote and recited to his wife, Diana (while Margarite patiently awaits his return to her).

The narrator, who has previously been relatively unintrusive, reports that these poems are included because they "gaue certaine signes in him of an excellent witte" (202). Regardless of the narrator's intention that these poems should demonstrate the breadth of Arsadachus's character, the introductions the text provides to the poems quickly change to stress the artistic and learned nature of the poetry:

> The third [poem] though short for the method, is verie sweete, and is written in imitation of *Dolce* the *Italian*, beginning thus: *Io veggio*, etc. (204)
> . . . .
> The fourth being written vpon a more wanton subiect, is farre more poeticall, and hath in it his decoram [*sic*] as well as the rest. (204)
> . . . .
> Another melancholy of his for the strangenesse thereof deserueth to be registred, and the rather, in that it is in immitation of that excellent Poet of *Italie*, *Lodouice Pascale*, in his sonnet beginning; *Tutte le telle hauean de'l ciel l'impere.* (206)

The cumulative effects of such comments, and the similar comments that introduce the remainder of the ten poems, turn the reader into a courtly, educated individual able to read the poetry in terms of its Italian source material, its literary technique, and the appropriateness of its subject matter. Like the prose comments that punctuate the eclogues of Sidney's *Arcadia* or G.T.'s evaluative remarks on F.J.'s poetry in Gascoigne's work, Lodge's prose introductions to the poems of *Margarite* temporarily transform his romance into high literary art, altering his position as an author (claiming not only the authority presented by poetry, but also that indicated by thorough knowledge of Italian poetry), and transforming his readers into university wits able to assess the poetry's artistic merits. Lodge's strategies here may also be understood as introducing into Lodge's text an element of intertextuality common to notions of mannerist play, but even if seen in the context of literary mannerism, the effect in Lodge's text is still the same: readers are temporarily placed into the community of aristocratic readers able to understand the relationship of *Margarite*'s poetry to its Italian models.[4]

Thomas Deloney's *Jack of Newbury* may also demonstrate the ways in which poetry is inserted into prose fictions in order to authorize their writers and their readers. Deloney's text, more well-known than Lodge's, describes the rise of John Winchcomb, known as Jack of Newbury, from the servant of a clothier to a member of Parliament. During the course of Jack's progress, several poems are presented to Deloney's readers, ranging from Jack's twelve-line farewell to his drinking companions (6–7), to the songs sung by Jack's weavers and servant women (40–47), to Will Summer's brief summary of his treatment by Jack's maids (52), to a poetic catalog of the signs of Jack's wealth (26–28). My purpose is not to discuss the poems individually, but rather to observe that they link Jack's rise to power with traditional literary genres—most notably the ballad—that contain whatever subversive content Deloney's narrative may suggest. Significant, too, in Deloney's text is that these embedded verse texts occur early in the work: Will Summer's ditty, located in the fourth of eleven chapters, is the last that appears. After the suppression of a traditional representative of misrule, the jester Summers, Deloney's text is able to assert its authority solely through prose. During the scene in which Jack attempts to organize his fellow clothiers, an embedded text is again used, but here it is a letter in prose—the new mode of the novelistic writers. Poetry contains potentially subversive elements in Deloney's text until Jack's power as a member of the merchant class emerges, until, in other words, the text moves beyond a need for traditional artistic forms.[5]

I

Lodge's *A Margarite of America* and Deloney's *Jack of Newbury* provide two brief examples of the possible effects of poetry's uses within novelistic discourse in early modern England. The best way to begin a more thorough analysis of the subject is by reference to Virginia Woolf's discussion of the uses of poetry and prose within Sidney's *The Countess of Pembroke's Arcadia*. In the course of Woolf's description of *Arcadia* as a novel (her term for it), she explains that Sidney's text entices its readers at first because of its language and alterity to our life but that it ultimately remains unsatisfying because it lacks cohesion. She describes Sidney's romance as a text that readers find off-putting because it is a web of stories without a center. (One wishes, at this point, that she had access to the more unified *Old Arcadia*.) Poetry, in Woolf's view, functions to make clear "the boundaries in which Sidney was working"; prose in the romance

> is made for slow, noble, and generalised emotions; for the description of wide landscapes; for the conveyance of long, equable discourses uninterrupted for pages together by any other speaker.... when Sidney wished to sum up, to strike hard, to register a single and definite impression, he turns to verse. Verse in the *Arcadia* performs something of the function of dialogue in the modern novel.

Woolf contrasts "the realism and vigor of the verse" with the "drowsy languor" of *Arcadia*'s prose.[6]

While we might quibble with terming such poetry as "Ye Goatherd Gods" realistic, Woolf's conclusion addresses two key issues: it acknowledges a fundamental difference between the function of prose and verse in *Arcadia,* and it recognizes the shift that occurs in the reading process when the text moves from prose to poetry. This shift—the conscious awareness that the expectations of the text are not being met—is fundamental to the operation of much Elizabethan novelistic discourse that employs poetry. For Sidney, as for Lodge, Deloney, Gascoigne, and Barnabe Riche, poetry calls into question the nature and limits of the prose text, requiring its readers to actively (if subconsciously) reassess the generic nature of the work.

In Gascoigne's *The Adventures of Master F.J.* (1573), for instance, the poetry foregrounds itself by claiming to be the true kernel of the narrative. Since the text consists of F.J.'s poems and G.T.'s explanations and analyses of them, the reader is continually asked to define "fiction" in terms of poetry: novelistic discourse in *Master F.J.* is that which is based on and explains monologic poetry. This system of expectations asks the reader to overlook the fact that late in *Master F.J.* G.T. provides the reader with information F.J. could not have known and, thus, could not have transmitted to G.T. For instance, G.T. reports conversations at dinners at which F.J. was not present, and he also describes private conversations between Dame Elinor and her secretary (and between Frances and Pergo) about which F.J. could not have known.[7] G.T. gradually makes fewer references to material that came from F.J.; but while he does assert more authority as the narrative progresses, he still maintains his distance from it.

The result of these narrative maneuvers is that the reader of Gascoigne's text is asked to give G.T. authority to focus on the nature of narrative interpretation and to give G.T. authority to tell his story because it is grounded in legitimizing poetry.[8] The text's authority is further grounded in the factual illusion Gascoigne's prefatory material creates. Gascoigne details the layers of the text created by the means of its transmission: F.J. wrote the poems, G.T. commented on them, H.W. edited F.J.'s and G.T.'s work, and A.B. printed the entire manuscript. The strategy of alleged factuality lends credence to the text just as the poetic foundation gives it an artistic base.

The artistic foundation of novelistic discourse in poetry is also seen—although perhaps less clearly—in *A Mirror for Magistrates* and Shakespeare's *The Rape of Lucrece*. These works, representatives of the complaint genre, claim no alliance with prose texts, yet their affinity to novelistic discourse seems clear. The ratio of verse to prose is certainly greater than in *Master F.J.*, and each poem operates as a more clearly independent unit. Although the moralizing purpose of the *Mirror* makes it a more obviously edifying text than *Master F.J.*, the prose links between the *Mirror*'s individual complaints unify the individual poems and create a structure which, in its emphasis on the composition process and on reflection on the complaints' moral content, seems somewhat analogous to the novelistic structure of Gascoigne's work. The group of poets who discuss, during the interludes, the quality of poetry and its moral significance act as G.T. does in *Master F.J.*: they shift the focus of the work from its content to the artistic process itself, pushing at the limits of poetry's ability to contain narrative in the modern world and aligning it with Bakhtin's sense of novelistic discourse as that which organizes extraliterary forces and multiple voices into an artistic form that may—or may not—be expressed in prose.[9]

The Rape of Lucrece (1594), on a smaller scale, similarly functions to problematize the nature of poetry's ability during the period to convey a narrative unaided by prose. The presence of the argument, which explains the events that precede and follow those contained in the poetic narrative, suggest that poetry, in this case, can function (to use Kittay and Godzich's term) to "monumentalize" Lucrece's rape, but not to explain its political causes and effects.[10] What we see, even in the traditionally established complaint, is an inversion of the relations between prose and poetry in novelistic discourse. In these examples of complaints, prose is needed to concretize and interpret the more abstract and literary verse; in *Master F.J.*, conversely, verse grounds and authorizes the text's prose. Because of shifting cultural conditions, neither work is able to authorize itself through the use of only one genre.

The traditional distinction between the complaint and prose genres may create resistance to this conclusion, and yet such resistance returns us to consideration of the fundamental difference between prose and poetry. The distinction suggested in the previous chapter is based on artistic status and economic constraints: true gentlemen creating "art" would be more likely to adopt the sonnet sequence, to be circulated in manuscript, than the prose of Deloney or Riche, which was intended for the bookstall. While some scholars accept an economically determined distinction, this separation between prose and verse is not universally accepted. Discussing early modern genres as a whole, Earl Miner erases the split between the two forms of writing: "western medieval matter well illustrates that prose and verse are alternatives to each other rather than matters classifiable as genres. There are romances in verse and romances in prose."[11] While significant exceptions did exist, such as Malory's prose and Thomas Churchyard's ballads, which of the two kinds of fictive discourse would have been more easily classified as art in early modern England and which would have been called "pamphlets" and grouped with cookbooks and herbals?

It would be wrong to argue that Elizabethan novelistic discourse presents a simple, linear evolution in its use of poetry. *The Rape of Lucrece* and *A Mirror for Magistrates* present one cultural response to the relation between prose and verse: from a culturally hegemonic position, these texts clearly subordinate prose to verse, a subordination possible because of assumptions about the complaint genre and its audience. Generic and audience assumptions for the writers of prose-based texts differ: poetry becomes increasingly subordinate to the prose links and the hierarchy is reversed. In romances, such as Lodge's *A Margarite of America* and especially in Sidney's *Arcadia,* the poetry provides a solid link between the text's readers and a traditional literary form. The poems quickly become, in effect, objects that act to motivate and move the plots of the works and not the means by which the plot is explained to the reader. In Deloney's *Jack of Newbury,* the elevation of the title character renders the use of embedded poetic texts obsolete, and they fade from the text, leaving its readers, like those of Gascoigne's *Master F.J.,* solely dependent upon prose.

II

In the novellas of Riche's *Farewell to Militarie Profession,* poetry is used in a fashion somewhat similar to that in Gascoigne's *Master F.J.:* poems in Riche's text become pieces of evidence to be discussed and interpreted much as any other physical object involved in his plots. Unlike the poems in Gascoigne's text, however, poems in the *Farewell* hold a much less central place; they appear within only two of Riche's narratives ("Sappho Duke of Mantona" and "Nicander and Lucilla")[12] and, while important to these texts, their presence is not as crucial as poems are to Gascoigne's work. Without Riche's poems, a certain degree of meaning would be lost, but the central issues of the narratives would remain coherent. The presence of poetry within Riche's text not only provides evidence by which the characters and their stories are revealed, but it also elevates the tales into literary texts, an elevation other of Riche's novellas achieve by alternate means. The poetry helps to remove temporarily "Sappho Duke of Mantona" and "Nicander and Lucilla" from the marketplace and insert them into the court.

The poetry of "Sappho Duke of Mantona," the first work in Riche's text, calls attention to itself much more explicitly than does that of "Nicander and Lucilla."[13] In "Sappho," the son of the title character woos a duke's daughter while in an economically subservient position (i.e., not knowing that he is the child of a duke, and believing himself to be an orphan dependent on the kindness of his beloved's father). Convinced that she will never love him, he, like the characters of Sidney's *Arcadia,* composes a poem about the agony of unrequited love in order to "conquer his affections" (39). Subsequently, he memorizes his verses, sings them to the ladies of the court, and causes his beloved to believe he loves one of her attendants. In other words, typical of the romance tradition, this poem is extremely self-conscious about its poetic nature, its artificiality, its conventionality as a love lyric, and its position within the plot to advance the unfolding love of the two characters (for, of course, the duke's daughter returns the young man's love).

The self-consciousness of this poem derives in large part from the romance tradition, but it also may stem, in a related gesture, from a need to establish the artistic authority not only of "Sappho" itself, the longest and most discursive of Riche's novellas, but also of the *Farewell* as a whole. Although Kinney calls "Sappho" the "finest" narrative in Riche's collection and has praised the parallel structuring of its episodes, Cranfill sees the story as displaying an awkward handling of the twenty-three sources Riche employs in the tale and rough transitions between its individual episodes.[14] Regardless of our perspective on the technical quality of the text, we must agree that its initial location in Riche's work colors our interpretation of it, providing a sense that the narrative desires to make overt the connection between the pamphlet and culturally authorized poetry.

The embedded poetry in "Nicander and Lucilla" also functions to link novelistic discourse with authorized genres, and it does so by addressing more clearly economic issues. Whereas "Sappho" called attention to its poetic texts as elements of the romance tradition, "Nicander and Lucilla" attempts to neutralize the artistic authority of poetry by diminishing our ability to read its verses as distinct from its prose text.

The argument of "Nicander and Lucilla," the third tale in Riche's *Farewell*, is as follows:

> *Lucilla*, a yong maiden endured with singuler beautie, for want of a conuenient dowrie, was restrained fro[m] mariyng her beloued *Nicander*, in the ende, through the greate magnificence of the courteous yong prince *Don Hercules*, the onely sonne and heire of *Alfonso* duke of *Farrara*, she was releeued with the somme of 2000. crounes, the which money beyng receiued by the father of *Nicander*, the mariage was performed, to the greate contentation of the noble yong Prince, but especially to the twoo yong Louers *Nicander* and *Lucilla*. (89)

This summary, while mentioning Lucilla's lack of a dowry and the money Don Hercules eventually provides for that purpose, ignores the motivating cause of Don Hercules's financial aid and the emphasis on economic and class status that provides the story's center. The opening passage of "Nicander and Lucilla" establishes Lucilla as a noble gentlewoman whose family has been reduced to poverty "by the frowardnesse of blind Fortune" (89). This fact defines Lucilla as the social, but not economic, equal of Nicander (if such an equation is possible). The economic inequity is emphasized by Nicander's father, whose desire for a wealthy daughter-in-law prevents the marriage both characters desire. Don Hercules enters the novella as a figure who acts explicitly on the harsh economic realities that govern Nicander and Lucilla's relationship: he sees her, desires her, and is rebuffed by her. Don Hercules responds to his rejection by convincing Lucilla's mother "to make Marchaundize" (96) of her daughter's virginity: in exchange for a dowry and his silence, Lucilla's mother permits Don Hercules to enter her daughter's bedroom and "abide with her as long as it shall please" him (97). When he attempts to seduce her, however, she refuses to consent and convinces him not to rape her. He is overwhelmed by her goodness, awards her a dowry although the bargain has been broken, and leaves her as if he were her "brother" (102). Only after these events does the narrative come to the happy conclusion its argument foretells. The text separates into three sections. The first portion establishes the mutual love of the title characters and Lucilla's determination to keep Don Hercules's sexual interest from upsetting Nicander. The second section—perhaps the story's most moving pages—consists of Don Hercules's attempts to strike a deal with Lucilla's mother and her anguished speeches as she tries to accept the economic necessity of selling her daughter's virginity. The final section consists of the bedroom scene, the Don's munificence, and the resulting marriage of Nicander and Lucilla.[15]

In the first section of the narrative the lovers employ poetry: Nicander sends Lucilla a verse-letter to ask why she has been avoiding him and to apologize for whatever unintentional offense he has committed. Lucilla, who has been hiding at home to discourage Don Hercules and protect Nicander from jealousy, responds with a verse-letter of her own. These two poems are not adapted translations from Giraldi Cinthio's version of the tale: the Italian narrative is entirely in prose. Neither Nicander nor Lucilla remark on the fact that they have written or received poetic texts. Nicander simply calls his poem a "letter" (91), and Lucilla does not categorize the genre of her response. The narrator terms Lucilla's poem a "sweete aunswere" (94), a comment that comes considerably closer to recognizing the artistic nature of her text, yet it still does not directly acknowledge the letters' genre.

Perhaps the refusal to refer specifically to the letters as poetry stems from the obvious genre to which the poetry belongs. The narrative, for all its emphasis on economics, is primarily a romance; its title characters function primarily within the conventions of romance, and, consequently, these poems seem to fulfill the traditional expectations for love poetry. Nicander writes in six-line stanzas that vary slightly the *Venus and Adonis* form,[16] and his language is the conventional language of the sonneteer. His imagery in the first two stanzas suggests the grief of the caged wild bird as well as that of the widowed turtledove and swan. The final four stanzas connect the birds' grief to his own loss and beg that Lucilla identify the offense he has committed so that he may clear his name:

> If no offence, but fond conceipt hath taken holde,
>   Condempne hym not, that shewes his giltlesse hande:
> Who hetherto hath neuer ment the thyng,
>   That iustly might against your honour stande.
> If giltie I, I ask no other grace,
>   Giue dome of death, and doe my sute deface. (92)

Although some subtle irony can be read in these lines (the source of the lover's complaint is not really his own "giltlesse" hands but Lucilla's *gilt*-lessness, her lack of a dowry), there is little else of technical brilliance about them. They evoke the courtly image of the mistress empowered to sentence the lover to death, but the language does not produce any startling effects—unless one reads a *double entendre* into the line "who hetherto hath neuer ment the thyng," which may then suggest Nicander's chaste desire as well as his inability to create vivid images.

Lucilla's poem seems equally unremarkable and conventional. She uses a series of seven modified ballad stanzas to try to explain her behavior,[17] and the explanation is itself faulty: she misleads her lover by identifying "heste of parentes will" (93) as the only cause of her actions. She echoes Nicander's bird imagery early in the poem, but whereas he referred specifically to a bird in a gilded cage, a turtledove, and a swan, she is only able to name the "birde which is restrainde / Of former hartes delight" (93). After that image she focuses specifically on her situation as she swears her love for and fidelity to Nicander. Eventually she includes the language of the union of lovers, common enough in traditional verse, which will develop into the tortured physicality of seventeenth-century metaphysical poetry:

> And there withall receiue,
> This pledge to cure thy paine:
> My harte is thyne, preserue it well,
> Till we twoo meete againe. (94)

But the quality of the verse is not the issue here; the socioeconomic implications of such poetry are. Because of the conventionality of Nicander's and Lucilla's love poetry, and because the two characters (and the text's narrative voice) feel no need to remark on its presence, these poems firmly establish the two lovers within the gentle class. These poems, especially the more obviously courtly poem of Nicander, define the characters as lovers in the Petrarchan tradition. Once poetry establishes the two lovers as members of the class likely to compare their position to that of turtledoves, the economic disparities in the text become more distinct and more disturbing. The poverty of Lucilla becomes more clearly unjust and, if we accept the narrative's attitude toward her gentility, more insignificant. Because these lovers are able to use poetry to align themselves with the courtly tradition and the conventions of romance, we understand their virtue, devotion, and the appropriateness of their marriage. Once these connections have been established, the turmoil of Lucilla's mother becomes more poignant: the match between the title characters seems desirable, and the eagerness to facilitate that marriage by whatever means necessary becomes more acceptable.[18]

Within "Nicander and Lucilla," poetry establishes the social— if not economic—class of the narrative's main characters (and, given the growing number of impoverished or reduced English gentry during the late sixteenth-century, it should be clear that there are ways in which social and economic class differ[19]). It erases historical distinctions between economics and status and assures its readers that through virtuous behavior economic lack is rendered insignificant. Poetry, in other words, lends authority to Riche's novella by firmly anchoring it in the romance tradition through its failure to see poetry as anything out of the ordinary: whereas Gascoigne's text authorizes itself by foregrounding the interpretation of poetry, Riche's narrative assumes that its verse will be taken in stride. These are two different authorizing strategies, but both rely upon poetry to establish their texts as literary art. The failure of the poems in "Nicander and Lucilla" to recognize their generic separation from the rest of the text downplays any sense of difference the reader may feel, such as that felt by Sappho's son in the *Farewell*'s first story when faced with the need to write verses. In this latter case verses are not seen as "art" by the writer although their audience perceives them as such: for Sappho's son they are instead a means of purging one's mind, a "physic." Equating conventional love poetry with prose, as "Nicander and Lucilla" does, erases the generic hierarchy current in early modern definitions of poetry and, thus, helps allow Riche's work to be defined as literary.

The authority the *Farewell* ascribes to itself through poetry also lends authority to attempts at self-definition by Riche and his readers. The poetry of "Nicander and Lucilla," as has already been mentioned, simultaneously emphasizes the centrality of the lovers' economic positions and argues that virtuous behavior erases economic lack. As the text stresses the economic lives of its characters, the reader—especially the female reader[20]—is forced to view a text from the position of either Lucilla's economic powerlessness or her mother's moral and economic dilemma. The position of Lucilla's mother, who remains nameless throughout the narrative, is particularly excruciating for the reader because it dramatizes an aspect of early modern marriage negotiations not usually portrayed so graphically in early English prose fiction. Her position as the broker in charge of the considerable economic power Lucilla could represent if she accepts Don Hercules's bargain reverberates throughout the text, prompting a possible echo of real possibilities in its readers' lives—prompting, in short, possible fleeting identification between Lucilla's nameless mother and the reader. Although these economic considerations provide the material core of the novella, they (in the form of the mother) are erased from the narrative's expressed values, visible in its opening argument and its closing lines. Before and after her function as bawd, the mother disappears; the moment of identification for the reader is denied both before and after it occurs, but it has nonetheless taken place.

"Nicander and Lucilla" provides a more complicated use of poetry than Riche's first narrative. Its lack of self-consciousness and the text's emphasis on economics combine to encourage the *Farewell*'s readers to see themselves as simultaneously part of the typical audience for romance, the class that, like Lucilla, must depend upon its virtue to compensate for its economic insufficiency and, like the faceless mother, that for whom romance conventions fail and for whom economic need is painfully clear. Riche uses these competing levels of identification within the text to make more poignant for his readers the failure of romance to address economic realities, the powerlessness of Lucilla, and the predicament of her mother. Her position insists on economics as the primary motivating force within the text; this force clashes with the courtly conventions of the poetry the narrative contains in order to disrupt the reader's sense of self as a consumer of art and compels the reader to see the marketplace as central to the cultural definition both of the self and of novelistic discourse.

III

Poetry within Elizabethan novelistic discourse exists within a spectrum of possible functions. As in "Nicander and Lucilla," it may appear unmarked, connecting the prose that surrounds it to the romance tradition even as it raises new issues of social and economic concern. When poetry appears in this guise, as it also does at least once in Deloney's *Jack of Newbury*, the texts and their readers are simultaneously elevated in class standing since neither needs to have poetry explained to them. Self-conscious uses of poetry—in Lodge's *A Margarite of America*, Gascoigne's *Master F.J.*, or Riche's "Sappho Duke of Mantona," for example—authorize their prose texts and readers differently: rather than assume that both may fully participate in courtly conventions, the poetry and its presentation is so structured as to emphasize its function and the proper means for its interpretation. Such self-consciousness is, admittedly, part of the Continental tradition of pastoral romance. Sidney, expanding on a tendency already present in Sannazaro, often structures *Arcadia*'s eclogues into poetic contests framed by prose analyses of the shepherds' songs. Nonetheless, such analyses of poems within novelistic discourse empower the readers of such texts, especially those readers outside the courtly audience.[21]

Poetry is not, however, strong enough to provide the sole authorizing strategy for Elizabethan novelistic discourse, especially during a time when poetry's ability to contain narrative—as our discussion of *A Mirror for Magistrates* and *The Rape of Lucrece* demonstrated—is beginning to be called into question. Other structural means for granting prose texts literary status must coexist with and amplify the use of poetry's generic power: the use of translations and the manipulation of narrative voice are two such techniques. The significance of these strategies has already been alluded to in discussing Riche's "Nicander and Lucilla" and will be explored more fully in the following chapters. The narrative voice's seeming acceptance of Giraldi Cinthio's praise for Don Hercules's munificence, we shall see, provides an example of the way in which Italian source material could provide authority for a text through diminution of the English author's role in its production.

2

Borrowed Authority

Appropriating "Italian Histories"

A POET, according to Puttenham's *The Arte of Englishe Poesie,* "makes and contriues out of his owne braine, both the verse and the matter of his poeme, and not by any foreine copie or example, as doth the translator, who therefore may well be sayd a versifier, but not a Poet." Given our previous discussion of Elizabethan literary theory, we can expand Puttenham's definition to apply in a limited sense to prose writers as well. It reflects, however, as Thomas Nashe argues in a typically extravagant moment, an idealized perception of the late-sixteenth-century process of literary creation:

> I must needes say, the descending yeares from the Philosophers *Athens* haue not been supplied with such present Orators, as were able in any English veine to be eloquent of their owne, but either they must borrow inuention of *Ariosto* [and] his countrimen, take vp choise of words by exchange in *Tullies Tusculans* [and] the Latine Historiographers storehouses; similitudes, nay, whole sheetes [and] tractates *verbatim,* from the plentie of *Plutarch* and *Plinie;* and, to conclude, their whole methode of writing from the libertie of comicall fictions that haue succeeded to our Rhetoritians by a second imitation: so that well may the Adage, *Nil dictum quod non dictum prius,* be the most iudiciall estimate of our latter Writers.[1]

As these comments demonstrate, both Nashe and Puttenham are critical of writers who rely heavily on the work of foreign authors. While Puttenham seems to dismiss easily such writers from the category of poets, Nashe's comments suggest a more ambivalent attitude toward authors who draw from classical and European sources. Nashe is simultaneously disdainful of them and, by implication, critical of his culture's encouragement of their tactics. The praise he sees given to those writers who use "no word which has not been used before" seems to imply that he has reservations about the desirability of modeling English texts on foreign works.

The two perspectives Nashe and Puttenham present indicate something of the complexity surrounding Elizabethan attitudes toward translating and imitating foreign works. While Puttenham is able to separate easily the translator from the true poet at the outset of his *Arte of Englishe Poesie,* his later discussion of English literature will not be able to adhere to this strict distinction. Discussing England's best poets, for example, Puttenham praises Wyatt and Surrey because they "trauailed into Italie, and there tasted the sweete and stately measures and stile of the Italian Poesie" and thus "greatly polished our rude and homely maner of vulgar Poesie."[2] He separates those who import the matter or invention of their art from those who merely translate or "english" foreign texts.

Both strategies—importing a writer's substance and translating exact passages—are used by writers of Elizabethan novelistic discourse as means of achieving literary authority. Like embedded poetry, which simultaneously forces readers to confront a literary text and empowers them to become interpreters of such artistic works, use of translated material similarly augments the authority of both the texts which employ it and its audiences by inserting both texts and readers into an established literary tradition. The general absence of traditional artistic authority underpinning early modern English novelistic discourse, the absence of a clearly defined market for fictional prose texts, and the range of issues these works consider seem to argue that such works would have to struggle diligently and in varied ways to achieve literary stature and autonomy. The appropriation of foreign material constitutes another strategy by which Elizabethan fictional prose texts were able to derive their own identity or, in the terms Stephen Greenblatt has made popular, to "fashion" themselves in response to "something perceived as alien, strange, or hostile," in response to a "threatening Other." Foreign texts, primarily examples of the Italian novella, function as one of many "threatening Others" Elizabethan novelistic discourse had to defuse in order to fashion not only itself but its readers.[3]

I

Riche's "To the Readers in Generall," the last of the three prefaces affixed to his *Farewell to Militarie Profession,* specifies the content of the work that is to follow:

> The Histories (altogether) are eight in nu[m]ber, whereof, the first, the seconde, the fift, the seuenth and eight [*sic*], are tales that are but forged onely for delight, neither credible to be beleued nor hurtfull to be perused. The third, [the] fourth, and the sixt: are Italia[n] Histories, written likewise for pleasure by maister L.B. (19)

While five of his narratives are "forged" from a multitude of sources, three are more specifically derived from Italian "histories" found in Giraldi Cinthio's *Hecatommithi.* Although Riche permits his readers to understand his indebtedness to foreign works here, he immediately complicates their response by asserting that he is not even responsible for the English adaptations themselves: "maister L.B." is their true English author. This confusion about the nature of the *Farewell's* authorship is further augmented by the fact that Riche's title page lacks any reference to either the English translator or the Italian author. Certainly, Riche is not alone among writers of Elizabethan novelistic discourse in creating a complicated relation between author, sources, and text (Gascoigne provides the strongest example of this tendency); he is not alone either in employing foreign material in order to create a series of textual layers that permit early prose fiction to achieve artistic authority. Examining translation's role in Riche's work, and in the period's novelistic discourse as a whole, will enable us to develop a greater understanding of the forces that drew these writers to foreign texts and of the culturally subversive possibilities translated material afforded both themselves and their readers.

Translation's role is crucial to any discussion of artistic authority because the use of foreign sources can be seen to challenge the literary control of English writers. No matter how skilled or gifted, a translator is always susceptible to the charge that he or she is merely working with the ideas of another or is merely practicing a craft, not an art. A translator is always susceptible to Puttenham's claim that he or she is a "versifier" but not a poet, an artisan but not an artist. Sixteenth-century England was filled with translations and translators, and their work exerted considerable influence on the development of English literature and culture. The studies of F. O. Matthiessen and H. A. Mason, for example, stress the desire of English translators to spread the influence of Italian humanism through translating Continental and classical works. Matthiessen goes further and suggests that translation was popular in Elizabethan England because the English "had grown conscious of [their] cultural inferiority to the Continent, and suddenly burned with the desire to excel [their] rivals in letters. . . . The translator's work was an act of patriotism."[4]

Matthiessen's formulation of the issues compelling English authors to translate may seem to suggest a desire to assert a certain degree of cultural arrogance, but it does capture an essential fact of Elizabethan culture. There was a desire, admittedly problematic (as many texts, for example Nashe's *The Unfortunate Traveller*, make explicit), to know foreign "things"—be they books or clothing or geography. This tendency suggests a desire to expunge the threat that foreign cultures posed to the authority and independence of sixteenth-century English culture. Moreover, it suggests a desire to eliminate this threat by posturing a relation of dominance to the foreign material, especially the non-classical and non-factual European texts the translators appropriated. Translated foreign texts, as we will see, presented themselves as alien objects, the contents of which would be viewed differently by English readers. Foreign texts could either be seen as imbued with unassailable artistic and intellectual (if not moral) authority, as were most classical works, or they could be read, as were collections of novellas, as texts to be augmented and appropriated for the sake of fashion. Works in this second category could be translated and added to the list of Continental items already deemed fashionable (such as foreign travel and the Italian books Ascham condemns or the popularity of foreign clothing Riche's preface to soldiers criticizes so harshly).[5] As Nashe's preface to *Menaphon* suggests, the impulse to translate foreign fiction seems connected to the urge to be chic. J. M. Cohen has suggested that a related factor spurred Elizabethan translators: the invention of the printing press created a great demand for books, and translation provided a convenient means to help satisfy that demand. Especially in the early Elizabethan period, the fashionability of the Continent allowed booksellers to market translations that they could produce fairly quickly (since Elizabethan education emphasized the study of Latin and French, making translators readily available).[6] They could feel relatively certain that their translations would sell to a public eager to be seen as fashionable.

There is little need to rehearse the variety and number of texts translated into English during the sixteenth century, especially during the 1560s and 1570s, when the interest in translating foreign literature was strongest. The freedom with which Elizabethan translators manipulated their source texts is also well known. Mason has referred to the best of Elizabethan translations as partaking in "a process of cultural assimilation"; Cohen states that English translators frequently "ignored their author's style and background, intent only on producing a book for their own times"; and R. A. Knox simply calls the Elizabethan translators' tendencies to eliminate or condense portions of the original (regardless of however competent the translations may otherwise be) "effrontery." It is perhaps best to define the sixteenth-century understanding of translation not as "effrontery" or as the close transcription of an author's intentions, but as characterized by the work of writers "inspired but not in any way bound by the original" from which they worked, a process Burton Raffel (writing about modern translation) terms "cultural diffusion, not translation."[7]

Critics writing specifically on translations of prose fiction, including romances as well as collections of short tales—such as those by Painter and Fenton—based on collections of novellas by, among others, Boccaccio, Bandello, de Navarre, and Giraldi Cinthio, similarly describe the freedom with which the English authors/translators manipulated their foreign sources. Salzman, Margolies, and Kinney have all noted the ways in which translators of novellas altered their sources by either adding a strong narrative voice that frames and guides readers through the foreign work or by providing analytical passages that interpret the text the English author presents.[8] Riche in general seems to resist overt narratorial intrusions that obviously guide, moralize, or interpret.

Two brief examples should clarify the breadth of possible means by which writers of Elizabethan novelistic discourse could recast foreign sources. George Whetstone's *An Heptameron of Ciuill Discourses* (1582), a work inspired both by framed novella collections (most obviously Marguerite de Navarre's) and by Italian courtesy literature, subordinates its six narratives to the discussions of marriage that form the core of the text: translated fiction only occurs as expanded *exempla* demonstrating various perspectives on gender and marriage. The most well-known story in Whetstone's work, "The rare History of Promos and Cassandra, reported by Madam Isabella," provides most of the essential plot elements for Shakespeare's *Measure for Measure* and is based on Giraldi Cinthio's *Hecatommithi* VIII.5. This novella is placed in the mouth not of an impartial narrator, but is instead told by a female character whose goal is to demonstrate what she terms the "treacherie" much more common to men than women.[9] The discussion the narrative prompts among *Heptameron*'s other characters shifts analysis of the translated text from the voice of an intrusive narrator to the text's fictive audience, which is unaware of the literary origins of the tale Isabella tells. The translated text, in other words, constitutes the source for continuing philosophical debate on marriage, but the narrative's role in the discussion is obscured through the means by which Whetstone embeds the text and by the failure of *Heptameron*'s title page or prefatory material to acknowledge its foreign debt.

Another extremely graphic example of Elizabethan translators' manipulation of source material may be seen in Angell Daye's translation of Longus's *Daphnis and Chloe* (1587), which includes poetry in praise of England's "faire Eliza thou of the heauens the care." Praise of Queen Elizabeth was, of course, common to literature written during her reign, and poetry in her honor had been inserted into novelistic prose before (for instance, in Anthony Munday's *Zelauto* [1580], a work in which it seems almost equally out of place). Like the eclogues in Sidney's *Arcadia* that seem to make specific reference to historical events, such as Philisides's song inspired by "Languet the shepherd best swift Ister knew," Daye's eight-page poem on the glories of Elizabeth's reign ("Not English shore alone but farther coasts, / Both of thy name and of thy honour boasts") calls no attention to its disruption of the source text.[10] The ease with which Daye could insert extended references to his country and Queen into the translation of a Greek romance, like Whetstone's silent use of Giraldi Cinthio's novella, indicates the varying functions of and attitudes toward translated material in Elizabethan novelistic discourse. In neither case does the English text suggest that foreign narrative is seen as an inviolable, authoritative body of material. Instead it enables a process of cultural diffusion that permits writers of early novelistic prose to authorize their enterprise through its appropriation by a variety of techniques, including use of another author's title or tale without acknowledging specific sources (as in Whetstone's text) or to further a specific, English cultural goal (as in Daye's).

Translation's role in the subtle process of cultural diffusion participates in the process Walter Benjamin describes in "The Task of the Translator," an essay that explores the reciprocal nature of translation—the means by which both the source text's language and the language of the translation are transformed by the act of translation:

> While a poet's words endure in his own language, even the greatest translation is destined to become part of the growth

of its own language and eventually to be absorbed by its renewal. Translation is so far removed from being the sterile equation of two dead languages that of all literary forms it is the one charged with the special mission of watching over the maturing process of the original language and the birth pangs of its own.

The continuing transformation of languages prompts Benjamin to state that "no case for literalness can be based on a desire to retain the meaning" of the original work of literature because literature depends more upon style than meaning and, thus, "a translation ... must lovingly and in detail incorporate the original's mode of signification" rather than its literal meaning. His emphasis on the vitality of languages, on their perpetually changing nature, and the difficulty of permanently fixing literary meaning helps to explain the vitality of Elizabethan translators and their lack of reverence for the language and perceived authorial intent of the works they translated. They were engaged in the process Mason emphasized in his discussion of sixteenth-century translation: the assimilation of other cultures into their own and, at the same time, the discovery of "native English culture."[11] While exploring foreign languages and texts, Mason's persuasive argument runs, English translators discovered the abilities and limitations of the English language. As suggested earlier, the invention of the printing press further spurred this investigation of the English language's limits and of cultural attitudes toward the authorization of novelistic discourse.

II

Exploring early modern perceptions of translation establishes a context in which to analyze translation's role in Elizabethan novelistic discourse and to attempt to address the specific issues with which this chapter began: the nature of translation in Riche's *Farewell* and the relation between Riche's failure to acknowledge the role of foreign texts—and their original English translator,

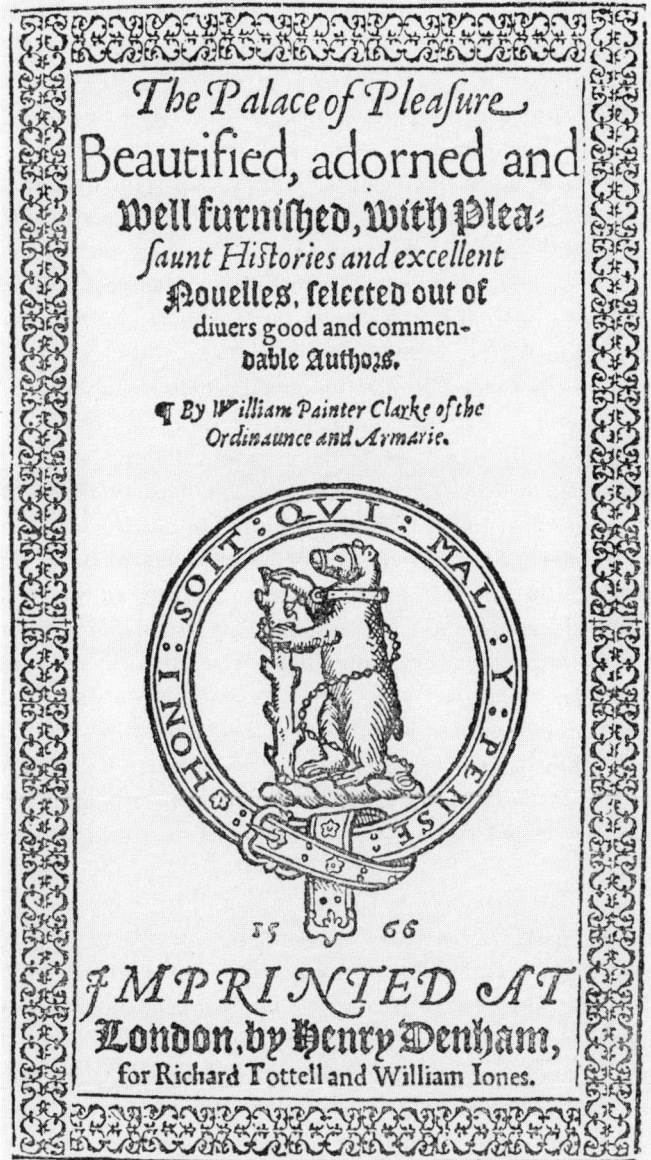

Title page of William Painter, *The Palace of Pleasure,* vol. 1 (1566). Courtesy of The Huntington Library, San Marino, California (RB 62835).

L. B.—on the *Farewell*'s title page and the establishment of the text's authority. One strategy by which to explore these concerns is to examine varying attitudes toward translation's role in Elizabethan novelistic discourse as expressed on the title pages of several fictional prose texts indebted to foreign material. The title pages of the first editions of the first volume of William Painter's *The Palace of Pleasure* (1566), William Barker's translation of Xenophon's *Cyropaedeia* (1567), Whetstone's *An Heptameron of Ciuill Discourses,* and Riche's *Farewell* provide a clear means for discussing the implied relation between foreign material and its English appropriation.[12]

Painter's title page from *The Palace of Pleasure* divides itself horizontally: the text in the top half identifies the content and authorship of the work, while the bottom contains the crest of Painter's patron, the Earl of Warwick, and the imprint. Both halves of the title page emphasize Painter's secondary role in the work's production. The woodcut of his patron's crest (which is amplified by Painter's lengthy dedication to Warwick) diverts the reader's attention from the volume's content or its author's relation to it to focus instead on the intended reader, the patron to whom it is dedicated. The top half of the page identifies *The Palace of Pleasure* as "Beautified, adorned and well furnished, with Pleasaunt Histories and excellent Nouelles, selected out of diuers good and commendable Authors." Then follows in the smallest type on the page: "By William Painter Clarke of the Ordinaunce and Armarie."

Again, like the bottom half, the top half of the page tries to diminish Painter's role in the work. Although the "diuers good and commendable Authors" do not receive top billing and remain unnamed, they do receive greater emphasis and a larger typeface than Painter himself does. Note, too, that the two words that receive the greatest emphasis (as indicated both by placement and type size) are "Beautified" and "adorned," terms that indicate how freely Painter has translated the tales of his classical and European sources. The title this half of the page ascribes to Painter is also of particular note. Either Painter or, more likely, his publisher wants the reader to understand clearly that his primary occupation

THE VIII. BOOKES OF XENOPHON,

CONTAININGE THE Inſtitutiõ, ſchole, and education of *Cyrus, the noble Kynge of Perſye: alſo his* ciuill and princelye eſtate, his expedition into Babylon, Syria and AEgypt, and his exhortation before his death, to his children.

Tranſlated out of Greeke into Engliſhe by M. William Bercker.

Imprinted Anno Domini
M.D.LXVII.

is not that of writer. This wish corresponds with sixteenth-century attitudes toward the incompatibility of gentlemanly behavior and publication within the marketplace, but it also helps to further distance *The Palace of Pleasure* from its author, as does the geometric border common to many Elizabethan title pages.

The title page of Barker's translation of Xenophon's *Cyropaedeia*, like that of Painter's *Palace,* also distances the text from its English author, creating a relation between reader and author that mimics late-twentieth-century notions of the conventions of translation. Unlike Painter's text, however, which deflects the reader's attention from its author onto Warwick, Barker's translation, through type size and spacing, focuses attention onto the Greek author and the process of translation ("Translated out of Greeke into Englishe"). This text does, however, shift some authority away from Xenophon by eliminating the Greek title from the page and substituting a typically lengthy description of the text's contents.[13]

It is, of course, impossible to ascribe intentionality to early title pages; they were the product, generally, of the printing house and not the author. Nonetheless, title pages do suggest a certain kind of "social energy" at work in cultural attitudes toward the ownership of translated texts: for Painter and Barker, authority is derived by deemphasizing their roles in the texts' production through attention to either the source text or the author's patron.[14] George Whetstone's title page, unlike Painter's or Barker's, fully elides the presence of foreign material in the text. Nor does it replace that emphasis with a focus on the English author. It is crammed with text that describes the subject matter of *Heptameron*'s debates and balances graphically the large print of the beginning of the text's title at the top of the page with the large type used to identify the printer, Richard Jones. Whetstone's name appears only once, three-quarters of the way down the page, where he is identified as the gentleman who has produced the "reporte" that is his text. Whetstone's title page authorizes its text through the philosophical nature of its debates on marriage, whereas Painter's and Barker's texts rely on the existence of "commendable Authors," either named or unnamed.

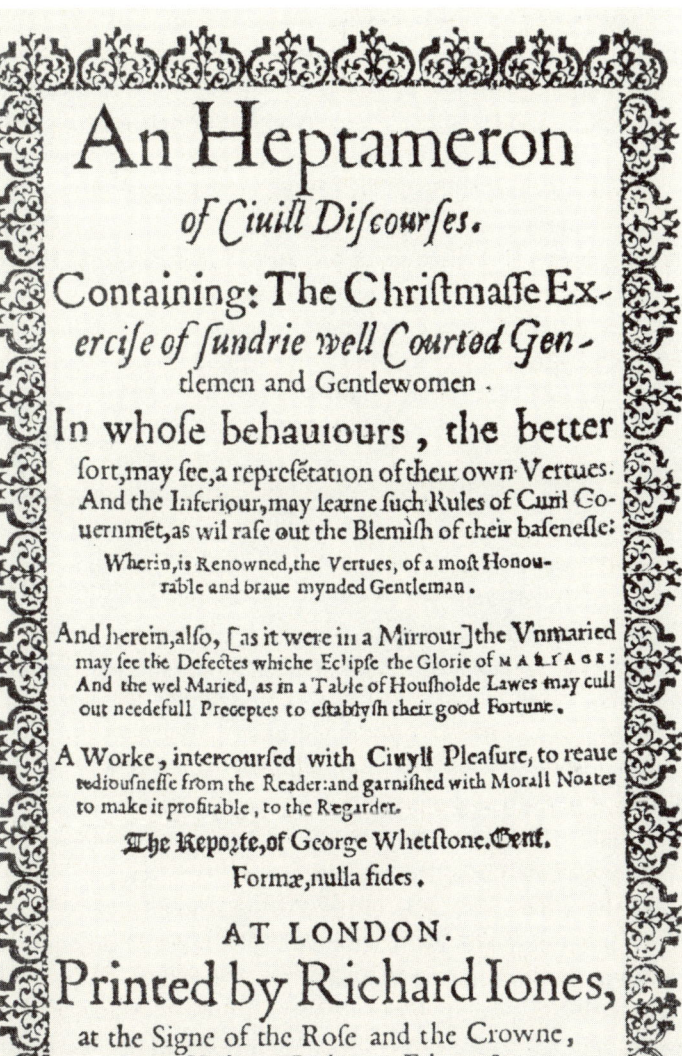

Title page of George Whetstone, *An Heptameron of Ciuill Discourses* (1582). Courtesy of The Folger Shakespeare Library (STC 25337, copy 3).

When placed into this nexus of possible approaches, Riche's title page presents a marked contrast to Painter's simple geometric border and its appeals to his patron. Riche's title page, like Whetstone's, alludes only elliptically to its foreign sources, and it presents an additional perspective on authorship and readership within Elizabethan culture. The *Farewell*'s title page, unlike those previously discussed, belongs more closely to the genre of emblematic title pages discussed by Corbett and Lightblown. Its very broad and active Moses and David border encloses text that is, too, markedly different from Painter's, Barker's, or Whetstone's. The most clear alteration is in the type size and location of Riche's name: "Riche" is both the largest and the first word we read, and no attempt is made to diminish the author's role in the work. Further, the title page describes the text without reference to any domestic or foreign creative assistance. The *Farewell* is described as "conteinyng verie pleasaunt discourses fit for a peaceable tyme: Gathered together for the onely delight of the courteous Gentlewomen, bothe of Englande and Irelande, for whose onely pleasure thei were collected together, And vnto whom thei are directed and dedicated by *Barnabe Riche* Gentleman." "Gathered together" and "collected together" are ambiguous and could suggest culling someone else's works as well as one's own in order to present adaptations of a single source in addition to novellas "forged" from the multiple sources (such as the twenty-three sources for "Sappho" noted earlier) to which Riche turned. Nonetheless, as on Whetstone's title page, Riche's eliminates overt references to foreign authors, and, unlike in Painter's case, there is no desire here to give Riche any title but gentleman. The work's title names his profession, but one that he is abandoning. Gone are all attempts to divert attention away from the author: the large block of print both begins and ends with a direct focus upon Riche. The placement of Riche's motto below the title again focuses the reader's attention on Riche as a person, a writer, and as an object of verbal play.[15]

Riche's title page makes no reference to L.B.'s contribution to the text or to the Italian materials L.B. is said to have translated. It seemingly desires its readers to see Riche as the primary focus of his text as well as its creator. Riche's personality is what matters:

Title page of Barnabe Riche, *Riche His Farewell to Militarie Profession* (1581). Courtesy of The Bodleian Library (Tanner 213).

it is because of his desire to please the gentlewomen of England the Ireland that the *Farewell* was written, and Riche is, his text seems to assert, entitled as a writer and a gentleman to appropriate material from English and Italian authors in order to produce a highly valued kind of translation—one that respects the untranslatable qualities of literature and adapts them in such a way that they come alive as vital works of their new culture.[16]

III

Consequently, the fact that three of Riche's stories were originally Italian novellas is scarcely significant, nor is it important that these three tales were first translated by L.B. What is worth investigating is why the foreign stories are included and identified as such at all. What does Riche gain by diminishing his responsibility for those texts, even to a minor degree? Still, before we dismiss the role of L.B. and begin to assign Riche the artistic credit for the translated tales, a few comments about L.B. himself seem in order. L.B. is generally identified as Lodowyck Bryskett, a friend of Edmund Spenser and resident of Ireland during the time Riche was also there. Bryskett is best known for his translation of *A Discourse of Civill Life,* the non-narrative portion of Giraldi Cinthio's *Hecatommithi,* and for accompanying Philip Sidney on his grand tour of Europe from 1572 to 1575. Cranfill presents a convincing case for Bryskett's identification as L.B. that focuses not only on his known translation of *A Discourse* and his extremely probable friendship with Riche, but also on the expanded references in the translated tales within the *Farewell* to Genoa, the city of Bryskett's birth.[17]

Cranfill's analysis of the translations also convincingly establishes their stylistic similarity to the remaining portion of Riche's text. Although the translated narratives may originally have been "written" by L.B., they have been adapted to conform to Riche's style and concerns. They diverge from the restrictive two-paragraph style of the original and follow the more expansive standards of the remaining works in the *Farewell.*

They are full of the repetitions and doublets that mark the style of Riche's other tales. Moreover, they show a much greater emphasis on characterization, motivation, and concrete detail than do Giraldi Cinthio's novellas, an emphasis consistent with the other texts within Riche's collection. Stylistically, it is very difficult to distinguish between Riche's original narratives and those that ostensibly first passed through the hand of L.B. As Cranfill has shown in his description of the frequency with which the phrase "ioye and contentation" appears in all of the stories of the *Farewell*, Riche has so thoroughly reworked L.B.'s translations that it is impossible to separate the work of L.B. from that of Riche, and the original Italian text has become little more than another aid to Riche's composing process.[18]

The existence of these three different authorial layers (Cinthio-L.B.-Riche) matters little in a literary analysis of the work. The extent to which the translations were freely altered helps provide a partial explanation as to why Riche, unlike Painter, felt no need to emphasize anyone but himself on the title page of the *Farewell*, and why we can accept the text as authored by him. But what does such freedom of translation suggest about Riche and his need to authorize both his work and his readers? The three stories Riche has chosen to adapt may suggest some answers to this question. Cranfill argues that Riche appropriates three of Giraldi Cinthio's best novellas to amplify the stories that precede and follow them within the *Farewell*, but a more detailed thematic consideration of the stories may indicate what value they had to Riche's readers and the text as a whole. The three Italian texts—"Nicander and Lucilla," "Fineo and Fiamma," and "Gonsales and Agatha"—are the third, fourth, and sixth stories of the work. They all recount the adventures of a pair of lovers who are separated and variously thwarted in their love until their eventual reunion and marriage. In this general schematic view they generally adhere to the typically comic pattern of the remaining novellas of the *Farewell*.[19]

What separates the adapted Italian novellas from the remaining narratives within the *Farewell* is the extent to which the comic marriages at the conclusion of the stories are allowed to prosper and, presumably, flourish. In Giraldi Cinthio's texts, the reader's attention is trained upon a single pair of lovers whose suffering and separation finally gives way to their reunion. In the remaining five texts of the *Farewell,* that same pattern is amplified to encompass a larger societal group. Northrop Frye's typology, on which I am cautiously drawing, suggests that domestic comedy usually concludes with marriages that involve elevations in rank and the admittance—"ushered in with the happy rustle of bridal gowns and banknotes"—of the major character into a new society in which the younger generation has replaced the obstructions of the old. Shakespeare's comedies, of course, form much of the basis for this pattern, and the groups of marriages that conclude his happiest comedies, most notably *A Midsummer Night's Dream* and *As You Like It,* suggest to many readers that the societies of these plays have been fundamentally altered by the actions of those characters whom society first ostracized and later valorized. Each of the three translated texts presents the resolution of the difficulties of a single couple, whereas the other novellas contain multiple love plots that suggest, as in Frye's paradigm of the comic world, the overthrow of an older order of society.[20] The use of Giraldi Cinthio's novellas problematizes that sense of societal reform.

In both "Nicander and Lucilla" and "Fineo and Fiamma" Fortune, rather than any systematic societal change, is central to the resolutions of their plots. In "Nicander and Lucilla" the two lovers, separated by economic status, are only allowed to unite by the munificent whim of Don Hercules, who decides not to rape Lucilla and instead to give her a dowry sufficient to make her acceptable to Nicander's family. In "Fineo and Fiamma" the lovers are kept separated by the determination of Fiamma's father's to keep her from marrying someone from a city subject to her family's control. Through a series of adventures typical to Heliodoran romance, both members of the couple are eventually imprisoned in Tunis, but they are ultimately freed and permitted to marry because the "teares of *Fiamma* and the onelie name of Loue" (118) prompt the magnanimity of the Tunisian king. There is, however, no indication that any aspect of Tunisian culture has been reformed or that Italian culture has itself been reconfigured to increase its sympathy to lovers separated by social or economic status. The presence of the "Italian histories" within Riche's *Farewell*, in other words, affords Riche an opportunity to question the shifts in social power other narratives within the text suggest are possible. In contrast to the world of "Phylotus and Emilia," for instance, in which the old societal order is clearly overthrown in the person of the jilted old man, the worlds of the stories drawn from *Hecatommithi* suggest a bleaker picture. In the Italian-based narratives, lovers are only reunited by Fortune or, as it would seem in "Gonsales and Agatha," an unsettling degree of devotion (or masochism, as feminist readers would more likely term it).[21] "Gonsales and Agatha" belongs to the genre of literature about the preternaturally devoted wife. The argument of the story establishes the issues involved:

> *Gonsales,* pretendyng to poison his vertous wife for the loue of a Courtisane, craued the help of *Alonso* a Scholer somethyng practised in Physicke, who in the steade of poyson gaue hym a pouder, whiche did but bryng her in a sounde sleepe duryng certaine howers, but *Gonsales* iudgyng (in deede) that his wife had been dedde: caused her immediatly to be buried. The Scholer againe knowyng the operation of his pouldei [*sic*] for the greate loue he bare to *Agatha,* went to the vault where she was entombed, about the hower that he knewe she should awake. When after some speeches vsed betweene theim, he carried her home to his owne house, where she remained for a space, in the meane tyme *Gonsales* beeyng married to his Courtisane, was by her accused to the Gouernour for the poisoning of his first wife, whereof being apprehend [*sic*] he confessed the facte, and was therefore iudged to dye, whiche beyng knowne to *Agatha,* she came to the Iudge, [and] clearyng her housbande of the crime, thei liued together in perfect peace [and] amitie. (148)

This narrative allows for no comfortable resolution, no easy sense that society can regenerate itself into a more just configuration through the influence of love, virtue, or honor. In fact, the judge before whom Gonsales is tried finds himself unable to administer any justice that would encourage society to diminish its need for individuals like Alonso. The judge admits that Gonsales deserves to be punished as if he had killed Agatha, since that was his intent; yet he is unable to execute Gonsales because Agatha is not dead. Nor is punishment what Agatha desires. Gonsales and Agatha reform their marriage and live "in good loue and peace" (165) for the rest of their lives, as is fitting for the end of a comic narrative; but it is a limited peace that does not expand its influence to any kind of social reform. Only Gonsales and Agatha benefit from her "vertue": Alonso is left to adore Agatha from afar and Aselgia, the courtesan, disappears from the text. As in "Nicander and Lucilla" and "Fineo and Fiamma," society remains unregenerate. The resolution of "Gonsales and Agatha" leaves its readers unsettled, and there is no reason to suppose that Riche's first readers—especially the gentlewomen of England and Ireland to whom he addresses his text—would have responded in a markedly different fashion.[22]

"Gonsales and Agatha," then, suggests a society unable to effect change on its members and one in which the only form of resolution possible results in the ostracism of the character most concerned with effecting that change, the judge who is prevented from punishing Gonsales. Such a portrait of society, shared broadly by the other translated stories Riche includes, provides a bleak contrast to the remaining five narratives of the *Farewell* that present a more systemic resolution to the problems of individual characters and a greater likelihood that their characters will emerge into a changed, more equitable world.

IV

Such a conclusion returns our attention to the relation between Riche's translated material and the authorization of his text and his readers. The distance Riche creates between himself and the narratives "written ... for pleasure by maister L.B." (19), although much less than the distance established at the outset of Painter's *Palace of Pleasure* and more considerable than that of the Whetstone's *Heptameron of Ciuill Discourses,* which refuses to acknowledge its sources, allows Riche to exploit the popularity of translated material and to figure himself (at least superficially) as an editor rather than a writer. This distance is somewhat diminished by Riche's repeated references to himself on his title page and by the stylistic similarities between portions of the text L.B. produced and those from which he makes no pretense of separating himself. Nevertheless, a slight distance remains. Once an ambiguous relationship has been established between himself and portions of his work, Riche is able to present the implicit pessimism of Giraldi Cinthio's novellas as a means of subverting the potential for societal growth and change the other narratives present. In the "translated" stories he can subvert the implied possibility for widescale social change contained within the *Farewell*'s other tales while diminishing his own personal responsibility for the contents of those translated novellas. The bleak societies they construct are not, he can always assert, his creation, but Giraldi Cinthio's ... or at least L.B.'s.

The subtle distance Riche creates between himself and these three texts permits his readers the same freedom. Because they have chosen to read a work whose title, title page, and first two prefaces make no reference to the translations the text contains (the first reference to L.B.'s role occurs on page nineteen), they are given an easy avenue by which to deny any desire within themselves to confirm the grim societal configuration that the translated stories, especially "Gonsales and Agatha," imply. And since these narratives are interspersed throughout the text, the readers are allowed the opportunity to shift back and forth between the social pessimism of the translated stories and the optimistic social reform of the remaining five. The translated stories work to contradict and subvert the ideological implications of the majority of the *Farewell*'s tales: that English society responds to its people's needs, that growth and change are possible, that reason—not whim—governs society, that justice will be served. The subversive message of these stories works to appeal to Riche's readers by responding to the insecurities produced by their economic status and their gender. The creation of subversive stories, such as these, helps those "embattled readers"[23] position themselves in relation to the economic and social classes above them, and to each other.

3

Constructing Voice, Subverting Narrative

THE MANIPULATION of translated material is closely related to the presentation of authorial and narrative voice within late-sixteenth-century novelistic discourse. As the separation of prose translations from their sources (or the near erasure of those sources) helped to authorize subversive critiques of the period's culture, so too did developments in the manipulation of narrative voice similarly permit Elizabethan novelistic discourse to enable its readers to question the culture's dominant ideologies. David Margolies's study of sixteenth-century prose narrative's response to the growth of a reading public and a print culture stresses the diminished or diffused nature of the author in Elizabethan prose fictions. As the writers ceased to fashion themselves as storytellers actively present within their works and became more anonymous personalities on the margins of their fictions, novelistic discourse became a convenient place for describing cultural assessments which "differed from or even attacked official ideology" as well as means "for embodying in a seemingly objective tale that which a prudent author would not say in his own voice."[1] Margolies's comments direct us to one of the most important facets of narrative fiction: its tendency to obscure its own mode of production.

Roland Barthes's description of narrative's method stresses the desire of fiction to distance itself from its author and to establish itself as an independent object. In "Introduction to the Structural Analysis of Narratives," he writes:

> our society takes the greatest pains to conjure away the coding of the narrative situation: there is no counting the number of narrational devices which seek to naturalize the subsequent narrative by feigning to make it the outcome of some natural circumstance and thus, as it were, "disinaugurating" it: epistolary novels, supposedly rediscovered manuscripts, authors who met the narrator, films which begin the story before the credits. The reluctance to declare its codes characterizes bourgeois society and the mass culture issuing from it: both demand signs which do not look like signs.

Barthes, of course, is referring to modern narratives and not to Elizabethan works, but as Bakhtin and Tzvetan Todorov, among others, have suggested, earlier narrative is just as subject to "disinaugurating" codes.[2] Even as Elizabethan novelistic discourse calls attention to its codes of production through elaborate systems of prefaces and seemingly overt authorial control, it simultaneously tries to disinaugurate itself from its foreign sources and authors in order to create an aura of objectivity and truthfulness about itself which its authors can then manipulate into the attacks on prevailing ideologies Margolies discusses. This distancing, however, assumes historically specific forms. In fact, as should become clear, one important way in which Elizabethan novelistic discourse establishes itself as a means for the critique of ideology is by seeming to use a historically grounded author or narrator to present factual information.

In order to describe the development of narrative voice within novelistic discourse that makes possible its critical stance, I propose to examine the split between the narrative voice and the authorial voice that develops during the period. While Riche's *Farewell* will provide the most extensive example of narrative voices within novelistic texts during the late sixteenth century, an examination of the narrative voices of Thomas Harmon's *A Caveat for Common Cursitors* (1566) and Robert Greene's cony-catching pamphlets (1591-92), which negotiate the border between fiction and nonfiction, will provide an introduction to the kinds of distinctions the period's narrative prose fiction will come to make. By noting the growth of a split between the authorial and the narrative voice within Elizabethan criminal literature,[3] we can more easily observe the parallel separation occurring within the period's romances and other novelistic discourse as well.

I

Before examining the nature of narrative voice in Elizabethan prose fiction, however, it will be useful to remember that definitions of narrative itself have become increasingly difficult to make. William Dowling, in his analysis of Fredric Jameson's *The Political Unconscious,* to take one typical example, stresses the existence of the narrative that an isolated "lyrical" moment implies as evidence of the broadness of narrative as a category and as evidence to support Jameson's assertion of narrative's primacy as a category by which we come to understand the world. Even a brief lyric, this argument suggests, reveals—through our interpretive attempts to establish the narrative situation to which it refers—our tendency to classify our experience as parts of a story. Citing L. B. Cebik, Wallace Martin concludes that narratives, "no matter how peppered with generalizations, always provide more information or food for thought than they have digested. Either they aren't worth interpreting (mere entertainment) or they engender too many interpretations." This state of affairs results from narrative's insistence on "temporal organization," rather than any notion of objective truth or singular meaning, as its fundamental principle.[4] Such a definition, which builds on the centrality of time within the novel seen within Bakhtin's treatment of the "chronotope," reminds us of the centrality of time within narrative, but seems problematic at its outset: the categorizing of some narratives as "mere entertainment" and, thus, unworthy of interpretation begs enormous questions about the nature of canon formation and the politics that surround narrative study. It would seem, as Jameson suggests, that although it may be overdetermined, narrative—including Elizabethan novelistic discourse—is more significantly seen as an epistemological category through which we attempt to organize and understand experience.

If, however, the temporality of narrative is merely a feature that helps readers and writers gain a sense of control over their lived and imagined experiences, we must dig more deeply to find a defining characteristic of narrative, a fundamental characteristic that will allow us to identify the subversive elements of narrative fiction. Such a characteristic can only be the presence of a narrative voice which must always be outside what Gerard Genette would term the "extradiagetic" level of a text's primary narrative. Reflection on events depicted within the narrative shared not with its characters but with its readers or listeners comprises the fundamental characteristic of narrative. Such an assessment qualifies Genette's definition of the extradiagetic. Whereas he would draw a distinction between extradiagetic narrators (such as the voice of Riche's *Farewell* or Deloney's novels) and diagetic narrators (like *The Unfortunate Traveller*'s Jack Wilton), I am uncertain of that distinction's usefulness. All narrators stand outside of the text they relate in as much as each must be charged with knowing that he or she is engaged in writing a fiction.[5]

Consideration of narrative voice and the degree to which it asserts itself is central to understanding fictional narrative; and the positioning of narrative voice within Elizabethan novelistic discourse is particularly significant as a means of developing a broader understanding of the fiction's concerns, its readers and its culture. Because of the novelty of the prose form and the problematic nature of its literary status, the period saw, as we have already seen, a great many structural and narratival approaches ranging from Gascoigne's layered text to Lyly's moralistic euphuism that devolves into a courtesy manual to Sidney's chummy relationship between his first-person narrator and the women who read *The Old Arcadia*. In addition, textual reception was changing greatly during the period and becoming fundamentally different from its medieval counterpart. During the hundred years following the arrival of printing in England, social and economic changes occurred that altered the way narratives were transmitted and received. More people—non-aristocratic people—were moving from rural areas into London and gaining access to various levels of education. Moreover, in addition to the greater emphasis placed upon rudimentary education, the influx of Italian humanism was increasing the value English culture placed on a classical education. Educational changes fostered and were accompanied by economic changes. Aristocratic and gentle classes were gradually losing wealth and status while the merchant classes were gaining economic power.

As more people learned to read, the number of persons reading narratives—as opposed to listening to them—increased. The growth of a reading public diminished one motivation for narratives designed for oral presentation: the mnemonic properties of poetry became a less important factor in the formation of narrative fiction, and prose began to assert itself as the form for extended narratives. As narratives became subject to individual readings as well as oral presentation, the nature of narrative voice changed. Because the fictions no longer required a physical presence to read them to an audience, the narrative presence of the *jongleur* became less necessary and authorial presence was freed to shift into a variety of forms.[6]

Walter Benjamin's discussion of Nikolai Leskov, in "The Storyteller," describes the central role narrative voice plays in oral culture as a focus of narrative attention and power.[7] Gradually, as oral culture is replaced, narrative structures need not emphasize the literal presence of a narrator and can instead become more subtle in their creation of a narrative voice. There becomes less need to address actively the readers/audience and to return their attention to the text being read, and there is less need to focus on repeated motifs and stylized settings, actions, plots, and dialogue. Because silent readers may flip back through the story to refresh their memories, complexities in approach, substance, and style are more possible. Such a process is visible in the narrative structures created in Elizabethan novelistic discourse.

As the individual experience of fiction becomes more common, the presence of fictional conventions is more readily posited and accepted by, to use Wayne C. Booth's terms, both the "implied author" and "postulated reader";[8] the more overt displays of "factuality" within fiction (such as the editorial layers of *Master F.J.* or Lodge's claim to have found the *Margarite of America* manuscript in a Jesuit library) become unnecessary. Still, the structural changes in Elizabethan prose narrative are not only due to the growing influence of print culture. Such an argument recognizes neither the structure of earlier novelistic discourse, such as Boccaccio's *Decameron* or Marguerite de Navarre's *Heptameron,* which create a network of fictional narrators, nor of either ancient prose fictions such as Apuleius's *The Golden Ass,* which presents a strong first-person narrator, or later novels, which create an author within the texts well after the reliance on oral culture has diminished. However, by foregrounding the shift to print literacy, we may come more fully to understand the loss of the rhetorically created author within the text and his or her replacement by what Booth terms "impersonal narration" that attempts to obscure the means of narrative production.

This simplification allows focus on the social and economic status of Elizabethan pamphleteers, their economic relation to their readers, and their role in defining for those readers the social and economic terms in which they could imagine and define themselves. The status of Elizabethan novelistic discourse as "pamphlets" and not literature, the aggressive location of the majority of its writers within the marketplace and not within the world of courtiers and gentlemen, and its emphasis on the lives and problems of the non-aristocratic classes all suggest that courtly readers of the fiction sought to gain from it something other than what they sought from sonnets. More significantly, its non-aristocratic readers found within it something besides what they found in other modes of discourse, something they were able to obtain, as we have seen, during their fleeting moments of class elevation during the reading of embedded poems within prose narrative. They were able to find a framework for understanding their position within and their attitudes toward the power structure of Elizabethan England. And writers themselves were similarly able to explore their position within their art, their class, and their society.

II

Thomas Harmon's *A Caveat for Common Cursitors* (1566) provides a good starting point for an analysis of the shifting nature of narrative voice within Elizabethan novelistic discourse because it presents a seemingly unified authorial and narrative voice. Harmon's *Caveat,* long considered one of the central texts of Elizabethan criminal and rogue literature, is presented as the summary of Harmon's discussions with criminals over a several-year period.[9] Harmon's conversations with the "wily wanderers" (110), as he calls them, yield a series of chapters, each devoted to the description of a certain kind of criminal, somewhat in the manner of the Overburian character, to which is often added a brief anecdote depicting the criminal in action. Harmon appends to his text a list of names of the three most common kinds of male criminals, a glossary of criminal cant, and a dialogue in slang accompanied by its translation into standard Elizabethan English.

The differences between Harmon's narrative approach and that Robert Greene adopts in his criminal pamphlets are clear. As we shall see, Greene allows the reader to doubt the veracity of his narrative voices much more overtly than does Harmon, and Greene even actively causes his readers to perceive a gap between authorial and narrative voice. Instead, Harmon repeatedly refers to his role as an auditor of criminal anecdotes, to criminals who have appeared before him when he was "in Commission of the Peace" (134), and to alterations he has made to the text since its first printing. Harmon's emphasis throughout is to present allegedly factual information in an impersonal narrative voice.[10] *A Caveat*'s chapter titled "A Kinchin Mort" provides ample evidence of Harmon's narrative approach: "A Kinchin Mort is a little Girl. The Morts their mothers carr[y] them at their backs in their slates, which is their sheets, and brings them up safely, till they grow to be ripe: and soon ripe, soon rotten" (144). The manner here is the language of definition. Harmon equates the slang term with its equivalent in Elizabethan speech then briefly tells us the fate of these girls. Although value judgments are certainly implied throughout, there is no way to separate the narrator's values from the author's. Both voices are joined here, and throughout the text, in condemning the criminal life to which a "Kinchin Mort" is exposed.

The most obvious way in which this text links narrative and authorial voice, however, is apparent in Harmon's alphabetized list of criminals, which presents the names of "the unruly rabblement of rascals, and the most notorious and wickedest walkers that are living now at this present, with their true names as they be called and known by" (146). Accompanying this list is no apology, no indication that naming names will endanger Harmon's life—a significant difference, as we shall see, from Greene's cony-catching pamphlets. Although Harmon has indicated elsewhere in *A Caveat* that information—including names and aliases—has been confidentially given to him, the text here suggests no split between the impersonal narrative voice that simply has information to tell and that of the author. This unified voice presents its criminal information without problematizing either the material itself or the writer's or reader's relation to it. Greene's pamphlets will create an entirely different situation for their writer and readers.

Greene's cony-catching pamphlets illustrate the kinds of definition and manipulation narrative voice allowed writers and readers to employ. Written in 1591–92, these pamphlets on London's criminal life drew heavily on earlier criminal literature, such as Harmon's *Caveat,* and they have long been considered to provide information about London life both by critics who stress Greene's familiarity with the kind of life the pamphlets describe and by those critics who stress the tradition of criminal and rogue literature that precedes Greene's work. The voice that presents the cony-catching narratives creates a complex web of responses to the material he presents; responses more complicated than G. R. Hibbard implies in his generally apt assessment that Greene "writes from the point of view of the citizen, but he does not like him."

Paul Salzman seems to be heading toward a more accurate analysis of the narrative voice in the pamphlets as he discusses Greene's "ambivalent moral stance." But Salzman's and other critics' emphasis on morality seems to place these pamphlets in relation to the "truth" they contain: it seems to suggest a desire to analyze these works as if they are factual instead of fiction, and it ignores the full implications of the narrative voice's relation to its author and its readers.[11]

The narrative approaches used in the cony-catching pamphlets do vary considerably. *A Disputation betweene a Hee Conny-catcher and a Shee Conny-catcher* (1592), for instance, consists primarily of a dialogue between two criminals, Nan and Lawrence, who discuss whether female or male criminals threaten England's stability more. In this text the narrative voice that seems to dominate most of the other pamphlets is replaced by those two characters, and only occasionally does "Greene's" voice enter to guide the reader's perceptions of the debate.[12] *The Blacke Bookes Messenger* (1592) is a first-person narrative presented by "Ned Browne," who tells us the story of his criminal life in the moments before his execution. The other undisputed pamphlets in this series (*A Notable Discouery of Coosnage* [1591], *The Second Part of Conny-catching* [1591], and *The Thirde and Last Parte of Conny-catching* [1591]), all essentially possess a similar narrative structure: abuses and crimes are described, criminal terminology is defined, and brief stories that dramatize specific crimes are reported by a unifying first-person male narrative voice.

The sixth pamphlet in Greene's series, *The Defence of Connycatching* (1592), is allegedly written by "Cuthbert Cunny-catcher, Licentiate in Whittington Colledge (11:41), who follows essentially the same narrative structure as the previous four but whose purpose is to criticize Greene for having described insignificant crimes (pickpocketing, linen stealing, purse cutting, etc.) when there are many more serious offenses to condemn. Grosart included *The Defence* in his edition of Greene's complete works, although he did not believe the work was actually by him. There has been much dispute about its authorship.[13] The fact that *The Defence* condemns Greene's works seems to have been sufficient to cause Grosart to reject Greene's authorship of the work, but it should not have been: the attitude expressed in the pamphlet toward Greene's works is entirely in keeping with the overriding narrative intent of the series of pamphlets as a whole. *The Defence,* like the other cony-catching pamphlets, is not designed to ridicule social problems or prompt social change. Instead, its objective is to represent "Robert Greene." Greene himself becomes the protagonist in this series, and the crimes he and his characters condemn are merely the means by which Greene attempts to tell his story. In addition, his presentation of criminal tales as fact is an attempt to gain authority for his art. By asserting the truth of what he writes, his art ceases in a certain sense to be mere entertainment (that specious category of narrative Wallace Martin describes) and becomes, superficially, social commentary that his readers can use to organize and understand their own experience of London life; it gains a kind of authority writers of Elizabethan novelistic discourse achieve elsewhere by use of translations or poetry.

In many ways, *The Defence* illustrates the trend in the pamphlets away from social commentary and toward fictionality for the simple reason that Greene "himself" is not present in the text to try to obscure our focus on him. Greene's presence as the narrator in the other pamphlets focuses our attention on the crimes he describes and the stories he tells: his readers see him not as character but as narrator. Only occasionally in those pamphlets does Greene let the focus of his writing overtly shift to himself. In *The Defence,* on the other hand, Cuthbert absorbs the narrative function and allows readers to perceive Greene as a writer and alleged social critic while Cuthbert ridicules him. *The Defence* begins:

> I cannot but wonder maister R.G. what Poeticall fury made you so fantasticke, to wryte against Conny-catchers? Was your braine so barraine that you had no other subiect? or your wittes so dried with dreaming of loue Pamphlettes, that you had no other humour left, but satirically with *Diogenes,* to snarle at all mens manners: You neuer founde in *Tully* nor *Aristotle,* what a setter or a verser was.

It had been the part of a Scholler, to haue written seriously
of some graue subiect, either Philosophically to haue shewen
how you were proficient in Cambridge, or diuinely to haue
manifested your religion to the world. Such triuiall trinkets
and threedbare trash, had better seemed T.D. [Thomas Deloney[14]] whose braines beaten to the yarking vp of Ballades,
might more lawfully haue glaunst at the quaint conceites of
conny-catching and crosse-biting. (II:49)

The vein in which Cuthbert begins here, that describing "setters"
and "versers" (two kinds of criminals described in earlier pamphlets) indicates some kind of intellectual weakness on Greene's
part, continues throughout the pamphlet. As Cuthbert turns his
attention to describing more serious crimes than Greene discussed,
he frequently addresses Greene contemptuously: "Is not this coos-
senage [usury] and Conny-catching Maister R.G. and more daily
practised in *England,* and more hurtful then our poore shifting at
Cardes, and yet your mashippe can winke at the cause?" (II:54);
"And are not these [brokers] graund *Conny catchers* Maister R.G."
(II:78); and, "How like you of this conny-catching [bigamy]
M.R.G.?" (II:94). The tone of these comments is unmistakable:
Greene is to be condemned for emphasizing minor crimes and
ignoring those that Cuthbert deems more significant. Yet, if
Greene is seen as the writer of *The Defence,* then these criticisms
must serve a different purpose than simply to provide social com-
mentary. If Greene felt the need to expand his scope, why not
widen his net in another pamphlet written as himself?

The Defence seems to enlarge the focus on Greene, a focus seen
briefly in other pamphlets. Had Greene simply written in his
own voice another pamphlet that condemned usury and bigamy,
his own role in the pamphlets or his relation to the world he
describes would not have been emphasized. In *The Blacke Bookes
Messenger* and *A Disputation betweene a Hee Conny-catcher and a Shee
Conny-catcher,* other narrative voices had been heard, but with
similar results: attention became fixed not on the condemned Ned
Brown who narrates "with a halter about his necke ready to be
hanged" (II:6) or on Nan and Lawrence, but on Greene himself.[15]

Greene prefaces *The Blacke Bookes Messenger* with a list of criminal slang terms that had been "lately deuised by *Ned Browne* and his associates, to *Crosbite the old Phrases vsed in the manner of Connycatching*" (11:7). This list is a veiled reference to Greene's previous pamphlets, especially *A Notable Discouery of Coosnage* and *The Second Part of Conny-catching,* which explicitly defined criminal terms and techniques for their readers. Ned Browne's list of new terms which should "crossbite," or deceive, the users of the old slang provides a way for Greene to emphasize his pamphlets' alleged impact. Because the terms defined in the earlier pamphlets have become so well known to the common Londoner, criminals such as Ned Browne have been compelled to devise new cant to maintain their air of secrecy.

A Disputation betweene a Hee Conny-catcher and a Shee Conny-catcher goes further to emphasize Greene's role in reshaping criminal behavior. In this pamphlet Greene's characters discuss his pamphlets and condemn him, in a manner similar to that of Cuthbert Cunny-catcher in *The Defence.* For instance, Nan states:

> I heard some [crossbiters] named the other day as I was drinking at the Swanne in *Lambethe Marshe:* but let them aloane, tis a foule byrd that defiles the [*sic*] owne neast, and it were a shame for me to speake against any good wenches or boon Companions, that by their wittes can wrest mony from a Churle. I feare me R.G. will name them too soone in his black booke: a pestilence on him, they say, hee hath there set downe my husbandes pettigree, and yours too *Lawrence:* if he do it, I feare me your brother in law *Bull,* is like to be troubled with you both.... I heare say R.G. hath sworne in despight of the brasill staffe, to tell such a fowle Tale of him [a certain criminal with the initials R.B.] in his blacke Booke, that it will cost him a daungerous Ionyt. (10:225-26)

Such a passage advertises the next pamphlet Greene may have intended to publish in this series, the "black book" which would provide names of criminals, as Harmon had done, and, presumably, lead to their apprehension. *The Blacke Bookes Messenger* also serves to advertise this unpublished pamphlet, but, in addition, it focuses our attention on Greene and on the supposed response his pamphlets were receiving in the criminal world. If Greene can convince his readers that his material is accurate enough to make Nan, Lawrence, and Ned Browne nervous, then Greene is able to establish himself as a successful, or at least powerful, writer with an accurate sense of social conditions.

Greene, however, does not rely entirely on his characters to establish his credibility. He concludes the debate between Nan and Lawrence with this paragraph:

> Thus Countrymen you haue heard the disputation between these two cousoning companions, wherein I haue shakte out the notable villany of whores, although mistresse *Nan* this good Oratresse, hath sworne to weare a long Hamborough knife to stabbe mee, and all the crue haue protested my death: and to prooue they ment good earnest, they belegard me about in the Saint Iohns head within Ludgate: beeing at supper, there were some fourteene or fifteene of them met, and thought to haue made that the fatall night of my ouerthrowe, but that the courteous Cittizens and Apprentises tooke my part, and so two or three of them were carryed to the Counter, although a Gentleman in my company was sore hurt. I cannot deny but they beginne to waste away about *London,* and *Tyborne* (since the setting out of my booke) hath eaten vp many of them: and I will plague them to the extreamitie: let them doe what they dare with their bilbowe blades, I feare them not. (10:236)

Greene thus becomes a character of vital interest for his readers: he is a man able to effect change in his society and a man whose life is threatened by the unpleasant truths he has to tell. It is, however, difficult to take the words of this narrative voice seriously. The publication of his criminal pamphlets does not seem to be hindered by these alleged threats on his life, and Greene's popularity does not seem to have been diminished any by fear of retribution upon his readers.

Criminals who felt that their particular schemes had been exposed could have claimed reason to wish him harm, but it would seem that they actually would have had reason to thank Greene as well. In *A Notable Discouery of Coosnage*, as elsewhere in these pamphlets, Greene resists opportunities to provide criminals' names and to describe specifically ways in which honest persons are cheated: he tells the story of a man who "fel among cony-catchers, whose names I omit, because I hope of their amendment" (10:31); he refuses to describe "Cheating Law" (which he claims to know well) by saying that "although no man could better then myself discouer this lawe . . . yet for some speciall reasons, herein I will be silent" (10:37). These pamphlets are clearly engaged in cultural work different from that of Harmon's text.

Although critics have seen a progression within Greene's series of pamphlets away from raising moral and political concerns and toward providing pure entertainment, their reluctance to expose criminals when we know the narrative could must suggest they have another goal. Were Greene's intent to provoke social change, explicitly naming names and providing details in his pamphlets, or giving his information to the government would have been more effective strategies. Because, however, Greene chooses a secretive and limited approach, our attention is directed much more explicitly toward him and the distinctions he draws between his authorial voice and his narrative voices.[16] These pamphlets allow for the presence of an authorial voice in a concrete and distinct way, a way very difficult to accomplish in other kinds of novelistic discourse. Robert Greene becomes a character whose life is threatened in these works; he becomes a repository of information his readers do not have and a character in the fictional world his narrative voices describe. The boundaries between fact and fiction merge so that Greene is transformed from an author of mere entertainment into a "social critic" whose material is largely inspired by fictional jestbooks.

As Greene uses social commentary to justify and authorize his use of fiction, however, public service no longer becomes his focus. In fact, Greene begins to share the culpability of the criminals he describes because he refuses to name names or treat the more serious offenses he allows "Cuthbert" to criticize him for ignoring. Since narrative control and artistic authority are Greene's foregrounded concerns, social reform constitutes only a backdrop to be manipulated in ways that allow Greene to develop his pamphlets' sense of voice, authority, and purpose. Yet Greene achieves this strength by attempts to manipulate his readership into believing his stories of crime.

Greene's narrative strategies place his focus and interests within a kind of transitional system of texts that allows him to remain present within the texts while preventing his readers from equating the writer of the pamphlets and the historical Robert Greene. The creation of Ned Browne and Cuthbert Cunny-catcher permits the reader to see just how easily characters can assume Greene's voice. Once that observation is made, the reader cannot be sure that the second voice is not the primary narrative voice, the authorship of *The Defence* becomes disputed, and a clear split between the author and the narrator is established. Readers, then, must confront questions about their expectations for Greene's pamphlets and must question (be it only subconsciously) their responses to the criminal exploits recounted. The narrative quality of these fictions encourages readers to see the criminal activity purely as entertainment, not as illegal behavior to be halted, and once that interpretation has been made, Greene has successfully subverted the conventional impulses toward legality and morality on which he based his original overt appeal to his readers.

Greene's method is similar to many works of Elizabethan novelistic discourse, especially those written in the first person. These works, such as Nashe's *The Unfortunate Traveller,* attempt, at least on the most superficial level, to convince readers of their truth while they simultaneously defy realistic or historical boundaries (as is apparent, for instance, in Nashe's conflation of historical events).[17] Nashe's text, in particular, presents a complicated case. Jack's voice stretches our perceptions of narrative authority: the physical positioning of the observer Jack during Heraclide's rape is, for example, a particularly difficult instance. How much could he have seen and heard through a crack in a wall? Such a question interrogates notions of voice and asks readers to struggle to separate the authorial from the narrative voice and to believe in the independence and the truthfulness of the narrator in a way that subverts our interpretation of the historical moment apparently depicted within the text. The third-person narrative voice, on the other hand, which creates more overtly a sense of "impersonal narration" (as can be seen in parts of Harmon's *Caveat,* or in the novelistic discourse of Deloney, Lyly, and Greene), attempts to create an aura of factuality through objectivity. Like much later fiction, it attempts to limit authorial intrusions and to control the reader's responses instead through the selection of narrated and dramatized events, diction, choice of narrator, and description.

III

Riche's *Farewell* provides another set of narrative strategies that combine the separation between narrative and authorial voices apparent in Greene's cony-catching pamphlets and the attempts at the seeming impersonality third-person narrative affords. Unlike Greene's narrative voices, Riche's techniques display not only his economic needs but his sense of his readers' needs and concerns as well. Moreover, Riche's techniques rely both on the presence of an oral culture and on the contemporary uncertainty regarding the social position of prose fiction in order to place himself and his readers in an untenable position. The prefaces and conclusion to the *Farewell* provide the most specific indications of the ways in which Riche positions his narrative voice and his readers relative to each other in order to subvert the definitions and relationships he has created. Riche's "Apolonius and Silla" also presents ample evidence of the ways in which the disembodied, disinaugurated narrative voice can mislead and subvert the reader's sense of characters and narrative events. By examining this tale and Riche's prefatory material, the subversive possibilities his narrative techniques afford should become apparent.

"Apolonius and Silla," the second text in Riche's *Farewell,* is probably the most widely known and studied of Riche's works, largely because of its association with Shakepeare's *Twelfth Night.*[18]

It contains the story of Silla, Shakespeare's Viola, who dons male clothes and becomes the servant of the duke she loves after a shipwreck. As in *Twelfth Night,* the duke, Apolonius, sends her as his emissary to woo a young widow, Julina, who falls in love with Silla in her male disguise. The resolution of the entanglements this plot creates (made more complicated by the arrival of Silla's brother, who is searching for his sister) roughly parallels that of Shakespeare's play, except that Julina becomes impregnated by Silvio, Silla's brother, and Silla is forced to bare her breasts to Julina in order to prove that she is not her lover. Apolonius and Silla do, eventually, marry.

During the majority of the narrative, Silla is disguised as her brother, Silvio. As in Lodge's *Rosalynde* and Sidney's *The Old Arcadia,* the narrative voice of "Apolonius and Silla" is complicit in the deception—or the attempted deception—Silla creates. Riche's narrative voice informs the reader of the motives for the transformation without making any initial attempt to obscure events:

> ... and now [after the shipwreck] to preuent a nomber of iniuries, that might bee proffered to a woman that was lefte in her case, she [Silla] determined to leaue her owne apparell, and to sort her self into some of those sutes [she had found], that beyng taken for a man, she might passe through the Countrie in the better safetie, [and] as she changed her apparell, she thought it likewise conuenient to change her name, wherefore not readily happenyng on any other, she called her self *Siluio,* by the name of her owne brother, whom you haue heard spoken of before. (73)

Given this knowledge, there is no "secret" from the readers that the narrative voice must maintain, and there is no need on the diagetic level for passages such as the following, which occur while Silla is disguised: "who but *Siluio* then was moste neate aboute hym [the Duke], in helpyng of hym to make hym readie in a mornyng, ... *Siluio* pleased his maister so well, that aboue all the reste of his seruauntes aboute hym, he had the greatest credite, and the Duke put him moste in trust" (73); "Poorc *Siluio,* hauyng gotte intelligence by some of his fellowes, what was the cause that the Duke his Maister did beare suche displeasure vnto hym" (80); and, perhaps most puzzling of all, "And here with all loosing his garmentes doune to his stomacke, and shewed *Iuliua* [*sic*] his breastes and pretie teates" (86).

Such statements by the narrative voice overemphasize the fictionality of the account presented. Riche's narrative voice in this story seems unwilling to accept Silla's masquerade but must continually call attention to it by the use of masculine pronouns when they achieve no narrative end and only the reader is in a position to be exposed to them.[19] The masculine pronouns suggest a narrative voice ill at ease with that role: a voice willing to present fictional narratives but which must continually emphasize its narrative role and establish its power by providing readers with unneeded information that serves only to problematize their attempts at interpretation.

Such a goal is also the overriding emphasis of the three prefaces and conclusion to the *Farewell.* These segments of the work present the most detailed picture we have of the work's narrative voice. There are brief authorial intrusions throughout the *Farewell,* but it is in the documents in which the narrative voice intends not to tell a story, but to define itself, that Riche's development of traits visible in nascent form in Greene's pamphlets becomes apparent. Splitting the narrative and authorial voice becomes of primary importance in Riche, and, as the narrative voice assumes the dominant role and essentially erases the authorial voice, it is able to strongly emphasize the nature of its readers and their position relative to novelistic discourse.

Riche's prefaces are addressed to "the right courteous gentlewomen, bothe of Englande and Irelande" (3), to "the noble Souldiours bothe of Englande and Irelande" (9), and to "the Readers in general" (19). These texts contain first-person addresses to the groups specified, and, while certainly much of their contents is conventional, each preface suggests that the speaker takes a different view of his narrative material.[20] The preface to women suggests that the narrator, although a soldier, realizes that it would be more pleasant to leave the military life and devote himself instead to pleasing women.

> Experience now hath taught me, that to bee of Mars his crewe, there is nothyng but paine, trauaill, tormoill, disquiet, colde, hunger, th[ir]ste, penurie, badde lodging, worse fare, vnquiet slepe, with a number of other calamities that haps I knowe not how. . . . Now contrary to bee of Venus bande, there is pleasure, sporte, ioye, solace, mirthe, peace, quiet reste, daintie fare, with a thousande other delites, such as I can not rehearse. And a man hauyng serued but a reasonable tyme, maie sometymes take a taste at his Mistres lippes for his better recompence. (4-5)

The preface to soldiers, however, does not reflect this positive attitude toward the work the narrator is about to present.

On the contrary, this epistle speaks bitterly of a culture that praises men for writing love sonnets and ill rewards those who are common soldiers.[21] In this preface, Riche openly criticizes the nature of the narratives he is to present, and he does so in a fashion that reaches beyond Elizabethan tendencies toward self-deprecation or artistic insecurity. Not only does he claim that his tales are of poor quality (in his preface to women he called them "rough hewen" [7]), he implicitly criticizes the spirit of the culture that is driving him from a noble pursuit (the military life) to the writing of fictions:

> And my good componions and fellowe Souldiours, if you will followe myne aduise, laie aside your weapons, hang vp your armours by the walles, and learne an other while (for your better aduauncementes) to Pipe, to Feddle, to Syng, to Daunce, to lye[,] to forge, to flatter, to cary tales, to set Ruffe, or to dooe any thyng that your appetites beste serues vnto, and that is better fittyng for the tyme. This is the onely meane that is best for a man to bryng hym self in credite: Otherwise I knowe not whiche waies a man might bende hym self, either to gett gaine or good report. (12)

The equation of dancing (a skill, he laments to his women readers, he does not possess) with lying and forgery suggests with what enthusiasm he greets the occupation he is about to undertake. Following this paragraph, we are presented with a litany of occupations the speaker feels are more honorable for a man. These professions—soldier, courtier, lawyer, merchant, farmer, and workman—are all seen to be unfashionable or corrupt, or too subject to society's whims. Having established English society's decadence and irresponsibility, he completes this preface with a short sermon on God's response to contemporary England and Elizabeth's role as savior of the country. Implicit within these sentiments is a feeling that by leaving the active life and choosing to entertain women, Riche is embarking on a profitable but morally worthless enterprise.

The brief epistle to the general readers avoids the issues the previous prefaces raised. It attempts to establish Riche as a gentleman who wrote not for publication but for the "disporte" (19) of his friends. Similarly, it apologizes for anything the reader may find offensive, and it asserts that his stories were "but forged onely for delight, neither credible to be beleued, nor hurtfull to be perused" (19). Such a statement removes the *Farewell* from the category of texts, like Harmon's *Caveat* or Greene's cony-catching pamphlets, that attempt to establish their artistic authority by claiming the veracity of their narrative voice. Riche's third preface makes a claim for the stories' value because of their ability to entertain and "delight." Such an assessment, however, must be read in the context of the earlier prefaces, which suggest that such amusement is a waste of the writer's and the reader's time.

The conclusion includes a tale ostensibly told to absolve the narrator from any charges that writing fiction is foolhardy. The embedded narrative tells the story of a devil who married an Englishwoman who was wholly preoccupied with her wardrobe. The devil becomes disgusted by her obsession with fashion and flees to Scotland, where he possesses King James's body (in a later edition, the devil's victim was changed to "the Turke"). The devil is only exorcised when told that his English wife has come to Scotland. Such a conclusion, which aligns literary and clothing fashions, undermines the value of the *Farewell's* narratives.[22] If all of Riche's work is nothing more than a response to literary fashion, and fashion is such a horrendous thing that it drives the devil back to hell, on what basis can its readers comfortably find any grounds for enjoying it? If they have enjoyed his text, then they are aligned with Mildred, the Englishwoman whose interest in fashion the devil found so repulsive; if they dislike Riche's text, or have found it to be the idle stuff of fashion, then they are aligned with the devil.

The *Farewell*'s narrative voice leaves its readers no solid ground on which to stand. Riche creates a series of prefaces that in effect challenge us to define ourselves outside of the bounds of the society he criticizes within his prefaces (we must neither be the soldiers with nothing better to do than read his work nor the idle women who provoke such wastes of men's time). We must define ourselves as outside of the economic classes who see fiction as a profession to be pursued in order to enjoy what we read. The individual narratives of the *Farewell* make self-definition difficult, as we saw in the inability of "Apolonius and Silla" to acknowledge the presence of its audience; even if it is possible, the conclusion removes the opportunity to maintain the extra-social self-definition needed to enjoy the *Farewell*. The text has subverted our sense of narrative and its role in society: it leaves no room for either the writer's authorial voice or the reader to exist within its world.

IV

What we have seen in this chapter is a progression in Elizabethan novelistic discourse away from an undifferentiated narrative and authorial voice to a complete disjunction between the two. Harmon's text presents unproblematically his criminal research and his unwillingness to acknowledge any overt contradiction between the implications of his narrative for himself (the author who is betraying many years of confidences) and the narrator who is educating the Elizabethan populace. As novelistic discourse in the period develops, however, the two voices split. In Greene's cony-catching pamphlets, for example, the separation between narrative and authorial voice signals a recognition of the writer's artistic insecurity and his need for self-definition in terms of social and political strength. Riche's narrative voice in the *Farewell* supplants any authorial voice within the text: it becomes impossible to assert the presence of a figure like Greene who exists outside of it. This narrative voice describes not only the writer's insecurities about artistic and social position, but it signals the reader's need to define him or herself in relation to the values of the text, values which—through the pronoun deceptions of "Apolonius and Silla" or the convolutions of the text's conclusion—the text fails to authorize. This lack of authorization indicates, even more clearly than do the "risks" the narrators of criminal literature take, the ways in which Elizabethan novelistic discourse uses its narrative techniques to subvert the ideologies its texts claim to present and authorize.

If all of the *Farewell's* readers are placed in the position of those of its conclusion and can adopt the position of neither Mildred nor the devil, what ideology does that text authorize? We are located in temporary alignment with the narrator, who is himself unauthorized by the text. In such a context, the *Farewell* is prevented from authorizing any established literary position: all positions in the text are rejected, and Riche's readers must develop a sense of authority for their readership based on their reading of the prefaces: they may either authorize themselves as the male readers who understand the limitations of the feminized culture the narrative voice laments or, more problematically, as the female readers who demand such frivolity.

4

Gender, Empowerment, and the Construction of Character

—

NARRATIVE STRATEGIES and voices within Elizabethan novelistic discourse, as we have seen, struggle to authorize a new relation between reader and writer, a relation that depends upon the gender as well as the economic identity of its imagined readers. Together with such nonthematic issues as the combination of poetic and prose forms and the use of foreign sources, narrative voice participates in the production of the cultural constraints placed upon both the writers and readers of the texts. The representation of female characters, the uses of description and the appropriation of non-European cultures, as the following chapters will suggest, further define the writers and readers of these narratives, but in ways that more clearly demonstrate the artificiality of a split between "structural" and "thematic" elements in narrative texts. As the following discussion will demonstrate, structural and thematic elements combine in Elizabethan novelistic discourse to describe the ways in which male authors represent femaleness. While they may be invested with varying degrees of power on the literal level of some Elizabethan prose narratives, women, both as readers of and characters in these texts, become invested with the traits of the "threatening Other" Stephen Greenblatt sees as crucial to the process of self-definition in the period. The figuration of female characters in these texts becomes a means by which male writers can solidify their own economic and social position.

I

In early modern England, the hierarchies of class and gender became increasingly polarized, as the experience of women and men, and rich and poor, became ever more distinct. The experience of women and men diverged: in wealthy families, women were less economically active; in poor families, the wage labour of women was different from that of men. And as the family became a less important part of local government and discipline, women's role in family government lost its public significance.... The divisions, which originated with economic changes, were reinforced by differences in education and culture.[1]

Susan Dwyer Amussen's description of the increasing power of gender and class divisions in early modern English society is an appropriate place to begin the discussion of the place of women in Elizabethan novelistic discourse. What she observes occurring in society is also rehearsed, in different ways, in the period's narrative prose. The economic and cultural changes she cites—the growth of capitalism that deemphasizes the collaborative nature of cottage industry and the centralization of government[2]—contribute to create new roles for women in literature and, perhaps more significantly for my purposes, new responses to the actions and ideas of female characters and female nature.

Amussen's comments are useful, too, in their emphasis on economics' central role in the culture's treatment of women, and her assessment applies as well to female characters in the fictional prose texts.[3] In the *Farewell,* for instance, at least two of its most memorable scenes emphasize the economic life of female characters. Lucilla's nameless mother, in "Nicander and Lucilla," and Messilina, the wife of Sappho, are both notable for the turmoil their economic deprivation causes: the first must turn bawd and the second must become a self-supporting seamstress. Women's economic life figures also in much other novelistic discourse of the period, such as Deloney's *Thomas of Reading,* Breton's *The Miseries of Mavillia,* Lodge's *Rosalynde,* and Greene's *Pandosto,* to name just a few. What seems significant about these examples, especially in relation to the historical conditions Amussen cites, is that in these texts women are represented as generally excluded from active participation in business life and its prosperity. Of course, the murderous female innkeeper in *Thomas of Reading* is an exception, and there are others, but female characters generally seem to lack direct access to the means of economic security and wealth. Although these narratives eventually achieve conventionally "happy" endings, their female characters are excluded from the economic growth possible for male members of the urban business class.

Much of this tendency can be seen as the writers' response to the simultaneous growth of the business classes and the aristocracy's decline. Riche demonstrates this decline through Lucilla's mother and through Messilina, but it is perhaps even more clearly seen in Deloney's Margaret, the aristocratic daughter of a fallen duke forced into a servant's role in *Thomas of Reading.* The prosperous citizen's wife occurs less frequently. She is present in Riche's "Twoo Brethren and Their Wiues" and in various forms in Deloney's works, but Elizabethan novelistic discourse seems, on the whole, relatively unwilling to explore the position of the economically competent citizen's wife; instead, it more generally focuses on female figures whose economic and social status is precarious, on figures who seem to be in the midst of socioeconomic decline.

What role do these female characters play in establishing the authority of both the writers and the readers of these fictional texts? Why, in particular, is Riche so willing to make his narratives' conclusions require the initial economic weakness of their female characters? This question becomes especially interesting in the context of the female readership Riche was striving to reach. Consider, for instance, the way in which Deloney seems to have exaggerated the economic and political strengths of his weavers and clothiers in his attempt to appeal to a "middle-class" readership. Why has Riche no interest in similarly exaggerating the economic strength or potential he might wish to ascribe to certain segments of his audience?[4]

To assess specifically women's position as readers of and characters within Elizabethan novelistic discourse it would be useful to look at three works: Lodge's *Rosalynde,* which contrives to present female characters both expelled from their socioeconomic group and yet in relatively comfortable control of their futures; Deloney's *The Gentle Craft,* with its prosperous and relatively independent women who seemingly determine their own futures; and Riche's *Farewell,* with its preponderance of impoverished or oppressed gentlewomen struggling to retain or recapture social or economic status. An analysis of the female characters in these works should help to establish the range of uses to which male writers put female characters and the range of responses those characters evoke. By developing a theory of how female characters are presented in Elizabethan novelistic discourse, we may be able to move to a broader understanding of the interrelationship between the attempts of popular Elizabethan male writers to subdue and control the ever-present female Other, the sense these writers had of their own experience of sixteenth-century English life, and the position of women within their culture.

In some ways, I would rather discuss works written by women during the period to reach conclusions about their position in their culture: I have more confidence in gynocritics than in the feminist critique, to use Elaine Showalter's terminology, as a means of uncovering and recovering female experience and perception. However, the body of fictional prose written by women during the period is small. Margaret Tyler's translation of the first part of Diego Ortuñez de Calahoria's *The Mirrour of Princely Deedes and Knighthood* (1578) and, if we move forward into the seventeenth century, Anne Weamys's continuation of Sidney's *Arcadia,* Lady Mary Wroth's *Urania,* and Margaret Cavendish's *The Blazing World* are the primary fictions known to be written by women.[5]

Study of these works would also be inappropriate to this study. My object is to identify the way in which a relatively new group of male authors created their artistic authority in the context of the dominant Elizabethan culture. Within that context, women function largely as a means of indicating to male society certain levels of socioeconomic competence and acceptance. Women serve in the period's dominant literary art (as in sonnet sequences, *The Faerie Queene,* and many of Shakespeare's plays), as means of representing (or causing) the success or failure of male characters and their social values. Elaine Showalter's "Feminist Criticism in the Wilderness" uses the work of Edwin Ardener to argue that women's experience in history has been "muted." This suppression has caused women's history (and specifically the history and experience of early modern English women) to be "mediated through the allowable forms of dominant structures."[6] Since women's experience has been distorted and altered by male control of texts, a study of those male texts can provide a more complete understanding of male perceptions of women and the function of women within the dominant culture. While it would be more attractive and, perhaps, more directly useful in terms of recovering women's history to study texts written by women, a focus on men's texts allows readier access to the period's dominant ideologies. Discussing male fiction in this context can elucidate the means of distortion and objectification of women specific to early novelistic discourse.

II

The prefaces to Riche's *Farewell* permit, in briefest space, the greatest insight into the range of possibilities for female characters within Riche's novelistic discourse. The first two dedicatory epistles provide initial contact with how Riche's narrator perceives his world and the range of his readers. Because these epistles have already been discussed in detail, only a few points merit emphasis. First, there is a marked shift in tone between the dedication "To the right courteous gentlewomen," and that to "the noble

Souldiours." The first document is self-deprecating in its praise of female readers. The narrator describes his military life as a period when "harebrained youth ouerhaled me for a tyme, that I knewe not bale from blisse" (3). Now, in his "riper yeares," he has realized that the nonmilitary life is more comfortable. He creates a sense of himself as ill-suited for the company of "ladies" since he has no interest or skill in music or dancing; yet, regardless of his inability to amuse women in conventional ways, he hopes his female readers will accept his "rough heawen Histories" (7) and encourage him to grow "from a yong Prince, to a sufficient Scholer" (8) of women's interests and entertainments.

The narrative perspective we see in the dedication to female readers has been studied by Paul Jorgensen, who ascribes Riche's popularity to his ability to address simultaneously male and female readers and, more importantly, to his ability to place himself in the literary role of the "blunt soldier" who is an inept lover. In this guise, Jorgensen contends, Riche carries on a literary courtship with his female readers. That the narrator has figuratively changed his professional role is further demonstrated by Riche's dedication to "noble Souldiours."[7] In this piece, the rationale for writing the *Farewell* is radically different. The speaker asserts that he wrote his stories "onely to keepe my self from Idelnesse.... But I trust I shall please Gentlewomen, and that is all the gaine that I looke for. And herein I doe but followe the course of the worlde" (10). Although he still hopes his work will please women, he denies that there is any merit in so doing: it is simply "the course of the worlde," what he will more openly criticize in the conclusion as mere "fashion." Gone from this account is any serious respect for what he is creating or the readers he desires (he had asked in the earlier dedication to be admitted to the congregation of his female readers and to be permitted to be placed "in the bodie of the Churche" [7] because of his devotion to women.)

The second dedication's tone is one of pure ridicule. The narrator seems essentially to expect his female readers not to read this document. He laments the frivolity of Elizabethan England, its lack of esteem for the wise and the professional (including the professional soldier); only wealth, he says, has merit these days. His disgust with contemporary England leads him to sermonize on the divine retribution due his country and to implore God to protect and guide Queen Elizabeth. He concludes without referring again to his book but finishes by praying that his fellow soldiers receive "better Fortune then I knowe the present tyme will afforde you" (18). The third dedication, the brief "To the Readers in Generall," resumes a conventional, self-deprecating tone that refers to the *Farewell*'s narratives as having been written "at the request of some of my dearest [friends], sometymes for their disporte, to serue their priuate use" (19). The stories are "forged onely for delight, neither credible to be beleued, nor hurtfull to be perused" (19). This preface asks readers to ignore the narrator's previous criticisms of his work, but, and perhaps more significantly, it also denies the overtly economic motive his earlier prefaces had established for the *Farewell*.

Two general statements emerge if we consider the role women are asked to assume as the text's readers. First, the narrator's ameliorating tone in the prefaces to the female readers and to the general audience is certainly only a pose: the remainder of the text will greatly qualify our view of the narrator's attitude toward women in each of these prefaces. Secondly, it is assumed female readers either will not read the preface addressed to soldiers or, if they do, that they will playfully engage with the text and will remain unoffended by its implication that writing a collection of fictional histories is evidence of the depravity of English culture (and the further implication that a desire to please women is somehow the cause of society's failure).[8]

The second of these two statements is more problematic. In the mind of Riche's narrator it would seem that women are not to feel the contempt the preface to soldiers seems to indicate, and the popularity of the *Farewell* suggests that women readers did not resent the implications of Riche's preface enough to prevent them from reading the work. In fact, Jorgensen's suggestion that part of the *Farewell*'s popularity may have resulted from the soldierly persona of the narrator would support claims for Riche's popularity with women readers. Such popularity may be explained by those who argue against a sizable female reading public: if women were much more likely to have Riche's *Farewell* read to them, then perhaps this preface would have been omitted by the presumably male reader. The problem with this argument is that the self-conscious nature of Riche's narration, as we observed in our discussion of narrative strategies, is such that we can expect Riche to have drawn our attention to such a desire. The preface to soldiers contains no direction to female readers or to those who would read to them: there is no overt marker to indicate their exclusion from this portion of the text. On the other hand, there is no apology at this point for having offended his female readers (and the apologies sprinkled throughout the text as a whole indicate that Riche's narrator could well have apologized if he perceived its necessity).

An apology might well have been called for unless we read the preface to soldiers in the context of Linda Woodbridge's *Women and the English Renaissance*. Her argument focuses on the documents in the formal controversy over the nature of women, but her central thesis, that writers in this debate were drawing on literary conventions and expectations rather than on any real women, and that these documents were read and appreciated for their skill in satisfying that set of expectations, seems valuable to our discussion. Although Riche's *Farewell* is not a part of this formal debate, it seems reasonable to read his preface to soldiers as part of this satirical tradition. If we assume that women could read this preface not as a personal attack on the uselessness of things effeminate but instead as a plea that all persons should know their proper place in the natural hierarchy and accept the responsibilities of their position, women readers could rationalize this preface into a neutral document that did not reflect disgust with a society motivated by women's "whims." Praising Queen Elizabeth in this preface masks its implied criticism of women. The limited praise Elizabeth receives (for rejecting the Roman Catholicism of her predecessor), disguises her inability to control the specific problems Riche condemns: London's decadence and a weak national foreign policy.[9] In this reading, the preface becomes a document designed to support the established order, and the problems Riche cites then become not intrinsic to any group but simply the result of not knowing one's place: the effeminate horseman wearing French fashions described in the preface to soldiers is ridiculed not simply because he is effeminate, but because his effeminacy represents a failure to maintain his patriotic position as an Englishman. It is not womanishness, but lack of manliness that renders him culpable.

But to assume female readers read this preface only as part of a literary tradition and were not more deeply affected by it seems to ignore the nature of the reading process. The tone of the preface, its suggestion that perhaps Riche would have been wiser to have remained "idle" rather than to be "ill occupied" (10) writing his *Farewell*, must remain present—at least unconsciously—in the reader's mind. It remains to suggest that the "delight" the stories can provide is a meritless pleasure, one for which, perhaps, the female reader is both aptly suited and one which prevents "manly" skills from being practiced. Female readers, it would seem, are given a great deal of power in this equation: they have the strength to keep Riche from developing his proper traits and skills. They, in essence, un-man him and render him as effeminate as the French-garbed horseman he describes. The prefaces give female readers the dubious honor of depriving men of their masculinity by merely being—and by being educated enough, and, apparently, vocal enough, to make known their interest in reading fiction in general and romances in particular.[10]

This sense of the woman reader in Riche's *Farewell* is not too different from Joan Kelly-Gadol's description of the mistress of Italian courtly literature.[11] The difference, however, is that Riche's female reader may not remain in the static position of seeming to determine the behavior of men in her society. The novellas of Riche's *Farewell* seem to require retribution for the power ascribed to women, and this retribution culminates by defining woman's nature as more fearful than the devil himself in the conclusion to the work.

Thomas Lodge's *Rosalynde* (1590) certainly does not reach the extreme conclusions of Riche's narrative voice, but it also—and even within the conventions of pastoral romance—presents a vision of female capabilities that seems to show their independence and strength but concludes by inserting them into a society as confined and limiting as Riche's. Its female characters present its readers simultaneously with images of freedom and entrapment. Rosalynd and Alinda, banished from court, seek refuge in the forest of Arden. There they achieve the freedom to support themselves economically (they buy a farm), and they have much greater control of their own futures (Alinda is free to fall in love with Saladyne—the brother of Rosader). Rosalynd, similarly, is able to court Rosader with a freedom not possible at court, but it is liberty which comes, as it does in *As You Like It,* Shakespeare's version of the tale, and in Riche's "Phylotus and Emelia," because she cross-dresses. Released by masculine attire from conventions of maidenly coyness and reticence, she is completely protected: she need not fear rejection (the kind of rejection which will send Deloney's Meg in *The Gentle Craft* fleeing patriarchal society), and she can determine the sincerity of his love for her.

Lodge's Arden is roughly as idyllic and as seemingly remote from patriarchal society as Shakespeare's, although some residue of the society's ideology remains. Arden allows Rosalynd to find a society she can control. Still, while Rosalynd is in the forest, probing Rosader's love for her, she has the power to guide Montanus's and Phoebe's love for each other, and she can nurture Alinda's love for Saladyne as well. She becomes an independent figure through her maleness, her seeming independence from any kind of economic limitations, and, ironically, her complete dependence on the patriarchal culture that has exiled her. Lodge has turned Rosalynd's punishment, caused by the threat the usurping king believes she presents to his power and Alinda's ability to succeed him, into the means of her independence. To cement her victory, the usurping king is slain in battle against her father, who is restored to power, and Rosader is designated heir-apparent.

Rosalynd's victory, her ability to determine her future and choose her husband, seems, at least superficially, more satisfying and less traumatic than the similar victory of Riche's Emelia. Riche's heroine also adopts male garb to gain independence, but for Riche's character there is no escape into a forest that is seemingly outside society. Rosalynd rules Arden, but it is a token rule, a kind of victory for Rosalynd that Lodge wants his readers to accept but which his narrative will not ultimately support. The conclusion of *Rosalynde* interrupts the wedding day to call Gerismond and the new husbands off to war because, as Fernandyne (Rosader's second brother) informs them: "hard by at the edge of this forrest the twelve Peeres of *France* are up in Armes to recover thy right; and *Torismond* [the usurping king] troupt with a crue of desperate runnagates is ready to bid them battaile. The Armies are readie to joyne."[12] The forest is not as isolated from society as it would seem: patriarchy governs here just as it does the Rome of Riche's Emelia. Lodge has led us to believe that some strength results from Rosalynd's adopting male dress, a view Riche seems not to share. Both the female characters of Lodge's *Rosalynde* and the majority of those in Riche's *Farewell*, however, experience society's constraints upon them in a more resigned fashion than, for example, Mistress Eyre in Deloney's *The Gentle Craft*.

The differences in the portrayal of these female characters arise primarily from the difference between romance and bourgeois fiction. The majority of Deloney's female characters (the most notable exception being Margaret in *Thomas of Reading*) tend to be more actively aware of and involved in the business that supports them. The strongest example of the powerful business wife in *The Gentle Craft* is Mistress Eyre, who devises the plan to buy £3,000 worth of merchandise, an act that gains Simon Eyre fame, income, and, more importantly, an invitation to dinner at the Lord Mayor's house. Admittedly, Deloney's narrator tells us that she devised her plans because "women are (for the most part) very couetous,"[13] yet it is hard to deny that she is much closer to economic factors than are Riche's female characters.

The Gentle Craft's tales of Long Meg and Gillian also further a description of women as "independent" of male control, although I say this advisedly since both Meg and Gillian are servants, economically dependent upon male desires, and since their goal is to obtain the love of Richard Casteler. The story Deloney presents of the attempt by Casteler and his servant, Robin, to trick the two women, and Casteler's final decision to marry neither of them, returns the focus to love, the focus common to Riche's *Farewell*. Robin is the primary trickster in this episode, and the women are only mildly abused, as we might expect in a text influenced by the jest tradition.

The only troubling result of the episode is what we learn of Meg's and Gillian's later lives: Meg "became a landresse to the Camp [of the king's army at Bullen], and never after did she set store by her selfe, but became common to the call of every man," and eventually, in her old age, she was "very penitent for all her former offences" (207). Gillian, in contrast, "was well married, and became a very good house-keeper, living in honest name and fame till her dying day" (207). Whereas Gillian is unaffected by her rejection and is willing to continue to conform to society's expectations, preserving her "honest name and fame," Meg chooses to reject the social conventions that have led her to pursue a man who did not love her and accept his tricks and rejection. Meg asks Gillian, "[H]ave I been so chary to keep my honesty, and so dainty of my maiden-head that I could spare it to no man for the love I bore to hard-hearted *Richard*, and hath he serv'd me thus? . . . never wil I be so tide in affection to one man again while I live" (207). Choosing to continue to support herself economically and emotionally, Meg firmly places herself outside patriarchal society. Like Moll Flanders, she only becomes penitent in her old age.[14]

The freedom Meg adopts for herself is unlike any position a woman in Riche's *Farewell* could assume. For Riche, female characters are too economically and politically dependent upon male power to achieve their freedom. Meg is, in a sense, an ideal Riche refused to acknowledge in the *Farewell*. Even Mistress Doritie exercises her freedom within the stable environment of her husband's house and his inheritance: her independence results from her marriage. Meg's freedom is unlimited by marriage, locale, or, significantly, children. Riche's women cannot escape the limitations of their society; they are biological beings bound by their economic status as well as, in many cases, their maternal nature. It would seem that economic freedom can only come to the married but childless woman, Doritie, in the *Farewell.* Meg does not need even marriage or widowhood.

III

"Phylotus and Emelia," the last story in Riche's text, presents female characters who are either economically deprived or socially constrained, but it also contains a male character who masquerades as female, thus making explicit some of the underlying male assumptions about the position of the female.

The novella describes the January-May relationship between Phylotus and the young daughter of Alberto, who is quite willing to permit their marriage in order to gain access to Phylotus's wealth. Emelia's brother, Philerno, who has not met his sister before the events of the story, disguises himself as his sister in order to prevent her unwanted marriage and, more importantly, to share a bed with Phylotus's daughter, Brisilla, before the ceremony takes place. He convinces Brisilla that she is to be married to Emelia's father and that the two young women must unite to prevent the consummation of their unsuitable marriages to old men. Philerno/Emelia suggests that they pray to Venus to transform one of them into a man so they can thwart their fathers' plans and marry each other. Philerno/Emelia volunteers to lose his "womanhood," prays to Venus, and (miraculously!) becomes male. He then embraces Brisilla, who perceives "in deede that *Emelia* was perfectly metamorphosed, whiche contented her very well" (194). The "real" Emelia, meanwhile, has disguised herself as a man in order to flee her father's house and join her lover, Flanius. Once the Philerno/Emelia-Phylotus wedding has occurred, Philerno/Emelia suggests that "she" and her husband should "trie by the eares" (195) which of them should wield authority in their marriage. The wife, of course, wins this contest and establishes the rules for their marriage. Eventually, Emelia returns to her father after Flanius has rejected her because he has seen Philerno/Emelia and is convinced that his Emelia is a devil. By the narrative's conclusion, of course, all identities are revealed.

What this story contains, beyond the disguised male and female characters dominated by their fathers, are several speeches by the disguised Philerno that present the arguments he deems most able to convince his father, and Phylotus, that he is Emelia; and, moreover, those he believes best suited to persuading Brisilla that he is first a woman and later a newly created man.

Philerno, having been raised apart from his parents and sister, has never met any of them before he appears on a Roman street one day and is mistaken for the disguised Emelia. Philerno acquiesces to the erroneous belief about his identity "to feede them [Alberto and Phylotus] a little with their owne follie" (188), and he makes his first speech as Emelia:

> Pardon me I beseche you this my greeuous offence, wherein I know I haue too farre straied from the limites and boundes of modestie, protestyng hereafter so to gouerne my self, that there shall be no sufficient cause, whereby to accuse me of suche vnmaidenlike partes, and will euer remaine with suche duetie and obedience, as I trust shall not deserue but to be liked duryng life. (188-89)

This speech comes shortly after the readers have been permitted to hear the real Emelia debate internally the benefits of her proposed marriage to Phylotus. The narrator carefully signals to the reader that Emelia's thoughts and rationalizations are developed in "a yong womans minde" (184): they are then presented— uninterrupted—for nearly two pages. Her actual reflections provide a means for examining so-called "real" female nature versus the "feigned" female nature of Philerno. She imagines a detailed chronology of what a day as Phylotus's wife would be like. A quotation from the pivotal moment of her thoughts represents a fair summary of the nature of her reflections:

> ... This likewise pleased her verie well, when she had supped, to vse some exercise, accordyng to the season: if it were in Summer, to goe walke with her neighbours to take the aire, or in her garden to take the verdure of swete and

pleasaunt flowers, this likewise pleased her verie well, when she was come in, and readie to go to her Chamber, a Cuppe of cold Sacke to bed ward, is verie good for digestion, and no coste to speake of where suche abondance doeth remaine, and this likewise pleased her verie well.

But now although she had deuised, to passe the daie tyme with suche contentation, when she remembred at Night, she must goe to bedde to be lubber leapt . . . all was marde. (185)

What is interesting about these two speeches is their extremely different focus: the first on form and rule, the second on practice and detailed life. Philerno's speech as Emelia focuses on filial responsibility and on the desire not to be "vnmaidenlike": it dwells on the outward symbols of propriety and seemliness. Emelia's thoughts, in contrast, dwell on the practical facts—the day-to-day pleasures and sorrows—of becoming Phylotus's wife. She concerns herself with thoughts of where she will go, how she will design her clothes, what kinds of food and drink she will enjoy. Philerno dwells on abstract definitions of female nature, definitions summarized and explained in detail in studies of the period's women.[15] An earlier speech of Emelia's (in which she begs not to be forced to marry Phylotus) also shows greater regard for the practical sides of life than for concerns with duty and filial responsibility. In that speech she admits that she does not wish to seem an undutiful and disobedient daughter, but that she wishes her father would "consider the harte whiche can not bee compelled, neither by feare, neither by force, nor is not otherwise to be lured, then onely by fancies free consent" (183). She acknowledges that the decision rests with her father but requests that he not marry her to "any that is not agreable to my fancie and good likyng" (183).

Philerno's speech to the fathers lacks any kind of detail that might be termed "realistic." It instead depends on calculations of what the two fathers want to hear—and how they perceive Emelia's role. It seems that Philerno/Emelia will construct Emelia's character in terms of her violation or adherence to rules of filial piety and obedience. Consequently, he develops an argument appealing to that set of expectations. When he meets Brisilla, his language changes, but it still relies on fulfilling conventional expectations, as if Philerno/Emelia is presenting himself *as* literary conventions. He develops a fictional story of Brisilla's impending marriage and of the need for both daughters to join forces to oppose the distasteful marriages their fathers have arranged. The "colde comforte" (192) Brisilla claims such a bond will provide allows Philerno/Emelia to discuss transformations of lovers reported in Ovid's *Metamorphoses*. It would seem that because Philerno/Emelia is able to evoke literary traditions (his disgust with January-May romances, the need for the daughters of doting fools to stick together, and the allusion to the stories of Lictus, Tethusa, and the transformation of Iphis), Brisilla is skeptical but not disbelieving when Philerno/Emelia is miraculously metamorphosed into a man.[16]

Were there any doubt about Philerno/Emelia's relation to literary convention, he proceeds, once married, to engage Phylotus in a Chaucerian *maistrie* competition, which he wins, thereby enabling himself to formulate the rules of the marriage, which are constructed so as to permit him to send prostitutes in his place to Phylotus's bed. This stratagem gains Philerno/Emelia considerable freedom, but the freedom in no way represents the options available for women. His empowerment is like that gained by Dustin Hoffman's character in *Tootsie:* he always had it. He uses a set of literary standards for how women should behave—or would behave if they were not suitably constrained by men—drawn from traditional works such as Boccaccio's *De Claris Mulieribus* and uses them to gain freedom as a woman and to tweak the old men's noses. The freedom Philerno/Emelia enjoys comes more from his male nature than his adopted femaleness. The actual female characters in the text remain relatively powerless: Brisilla is able to carry on an illicit affair in her father's own house, but the conclusion of the narrative does not permit her any anger at Philerno/Emelia for his "miraculous" transformation and his deception of her. Instead, Phylotus simply acknowledges that he has been tricked and allows his daughter to wed Philerno. Conventional expectations are subverted here: compare Phylotus's response to his daughter's deceit to that of the Duke of Vasconia in "Sappho Duke of Mantona," who threatens the man who has married his daughter without proper consent with the legal penalty of death.[17] Emelia herself also suffers at the hands of the sense of female nature presented by Philerno and the narrative. This is most obviously apparent in Philerno's ability to usurp her name and her life. Philerno/Emelia's behavior, however, also acts to deny her existence as well: Flanius, Emelia's lover, becomes convinced that she cannot be Emelia and that she must be a devil. Emelia is forced out of her lover's lodgings and into the street because Philerno/Emelia has gained primacy in her role. She must wander the streets of Rome for "three or fower daies" (199) until she gathers the courage to return to her father's house. Her speech upon her return deserves comment, because it illustrates the contrast between the language of patriarchal law and obedience and that of female nature. Emelia's first speech to her father is like Philerno/Emelia's speech quoted above. Emelia says, "I know I haue offended, and so farre as my facte deserueth, rather to be punished then pitied: the reme[m]braunce whereof is so lothsome vnto me, that I feare to call you the name of father, hauing shewed my self so vnworthie a daughter" (199). These words, which define roles and obligations, evoke "natural affection" (199) in Alberto, but they also prompt him to misinterpret her purpose. He believes that she is apologizing for disguising herself as a man; instead, she understands her fault to be having married Flanius without her father's consent. Meaning breaks down here: the only sense Alberto will derive from her speech—that there is some trouble with Phylotus—cannot be true. The presence of Philerno/Emelia has bereft Emelia of her ability to speak to her father, just as it has, in Flanius's eyes, prevented her from existing. Only when Philerno/Emelia relinquishes his claim to "Emelia" can Emelia return to existence, and only then can she again be understood.

In other words, female nature is defined in this text as a male and literary construct: Philerno can adopt it at will and convince other characters—both male and female alike—of his "femaleness" by his adherence to literary conventions of male expectations of women and of female desires. Emelia and Brisilla present two additional aspects of this definition: Emelia literally ceases to exist and becomes a devil when there is a competing, male definition of her femaleness; Brisilla is overpowered by the conventions Philerno/Emelia presents to her so that she questions neither his femaleness, his maleness (once she has felt his embrace), nor his blatant deception of her. As a result, the sense of femaleness that emerges from this narrative is one that male expectations determine and one that responds to female issues and concerns only as they are presented through male characters.

Regardless of the interrelation between male and female in "Phylotus and Emelia," the female remains Greenblatt's "threatening Other" relative to the male subject, and the two do not merge. Instead, the male characters and narrative voice appropriate the Other, emulate it, and so neutralize it. "Phylotus and Emelia" presents a rather successful appropriation of the female for male purposes. The only obvious problem with the attempt to control the female is the female ends that are accomplished: Emelia does avoid a marriage to Phylotus, and her escape to Flanius was neither enabled nor prevented by Philerno/Emelia's arrival, regardless of the narrative's attempt to suggest a larger role for him. In other words, this story simultaneously suggests the possibility of male containment of the female, but it acknowledges as well that such power does not exist. Youth triumphs over age, and (in part) female triumphs over male nature. That female desires only succeed when disguised as male (e.g., Emelia's flight to Flanius) or when they are really the desires of male characters in drag, suggests the limits of female appropriation and of the definition of female desire. Women in this text are known and taken seriously only if they are actually men, are disguised as men, or are not contradicted by men. "Phylotus and Emelia" suggests that it is difficult to ensure that none of those conditions will prevail. Conventional conceptions of female nature and desire, this story suggests, only work in male hands.

This conclusion is troubling. It suggests that "Phylotus and Emelia" defines its readers by reminding them of the power of cultural traditions and the use to which they can be put when faced with growing numbers of shopkeeping women and women readers. As a text for female readers, it suggests the need for the

Philernos of the world in order to achieve their desires: it reinforces the power of male readers and the dependency of female readers on them.

Other narratives within Riche's *Farewell* similarly reinforce a definition of female nature as dependent upon male action or initiative, although only "Phylotus and Emelia" uses a crossdressing male figure to create such a strong impression of woman as the projection of male power. The preface to female readers establishes female nature as the arbiter of taste, although it qualifies this sense by presenting its attitude toward women as a literary stance (a position confirmed by the letter to soldiers). A few of Riche's tales claim to present female characters who act independently of any male sense of their nature, but these female characters (Messilina, Lucilla, Isabell) do not initiate action as much as they respond to conditions male characters establish for them—the abandonment of Messilina and her daughter prompt her cleverness in business and contractual matters; Lucilla's final happiness depends not on her arguments to Don Hercules, but rather on his decision not to rape her; Isabell is in a position to save her husband and Tolosia only because he has "determined" her nature and exiled her accordingly. The collection's remaining works do present female characters in a seemingly self-defining position, but there is always (it seems) a catch: Silla only achieves power through male dress; Agatha seems to control her response to her situation, but her response is only effectual because of her support by Alonso.

The exception in the *Farewell*, the only female character who seems able to determine her own behavior or carry through her desires, is Mistress Doritie in "Twoo Brethren and their Wiues," who juggles a husband and two lovers until she decides to reject both lovers for a third. After her third lover has gone to war, Doritic lives "orderly, and faithfully with her housband, al the rest of her life, and her housebande who neuer vnderstoode any of these actions loued her dearely to his diyng daie" (146). The primary quality that enables Doritie to control her life is her location not in an aristocratic or noble household but in a world akin to that of Deloney's fiction. She is married to a man who, having inherited all of his father's possessions is able to live at ease. Nonetheless, doctors and lawyers figure easily in her world; letters between lovers are written in this story in prose, not in the verse of the love letters of "Nicander and Lucilla." This is a narrative world in which a large basket of "stuffe" (141) can be used to conceal a lover (much as in the buck-basket episode in *The Merry Wives of Windsor*).[18] In other words, it seems that the specificity of detail in this narrative, as well as its seemingly nonaristocratic setting, separates it from the world of the other texts that comprise the *Farewell* and permits its female character a greater sense of self-definition. But notice that Doritie poses a greater threat than do any of Riche's other female characters: she controls her relationships to husband and lovers, and her husband remains ignorant of his own cuckolding.

The more common model in Riche, more common even than the oppression of Emelia, is a focus on female characters—especially mothers—whose entrapment by their society is graphically depicted. Lucilla's mother in "Nicander and Lucilla" and Isabell in "Aramanthus Born a Leper" provide the most memorable examples. The inability of Lucilla's mother to maintain a satisfactory economic level leads her to pimp for her daughter in exchange for a dowry. Isabell's predicament is much more complex. She has been exiled by her husband, the king of Tolosia, on the grounds that her second child is the product of adultery; in exile, she acts as cook and housekeeper for a band of wrongly accused outlaws until she learns that Tolosia has been invaded and her husband imprisoned. She then leaves her nursing infant with the outlaws, returns in disguise to court, finagles her way into the jail nightly and breast-feeds her imprisoned husband to keep him from starvation. She becomes, in other words, mother to virtually all her society, and it is, significantly, through her agency that peace is achieved and the outlaws are reintegrated into the narrative's community. The graphic way Riche describes her inserting her breast between the bars of her husband's cell seems to suggest dissatisfaction—or an extreme degree of anxiety—about the amount of power the maternal Isabell wields: "She would leane her self cloase to the grate, and thrustyng in her Teate betwene the

Irons, the kyng learned againe to sucke, and thus she dieted him a long season" (175).[19] She is expelled from court, in essence, because of the anxiety the above passage suggests about maternal power and its potential to be abused: it can destroy the royal line of succession. Riche acknowledges female maternal power but makes Isabell pay for that strength.

Emelia and the other unmarried women in Riche's *Farewell* lack the power of Isabell (or Lucilla's mother, who can sell her daughter, or even Messilina, who can repeatedly contrive to escape from male constraints). Mistress Doritie lacks children but possesses power and the independence that Riche's mothers do not have. Her sexual knowledge and desire for adventure present her with ideal conditions for assuming control of her life, and the economic sufficiency of her husband prevents her from feeling any constraints. Her childlessness gives her the freedom equivalent to that of Deloney's business-class wives and widows. Yet, it is a temporary freedom for women within Riche's text. The seeming independence of Doritie is followed by the poisonous constraint of "Gonsales and Agatha."

IV

Unlike Lodge and Deloney, whose female characters are authorized by their texts' literal levels to achieve a certain degree of independence from societal control, Riche created female characters more fully limited by patriarchy. Mistress Doritie seems to be the exception. She appears to be a forerunner of the powerful business-class women Deloney would soon create—the childless married or widowed woman knowledgeable of business matters. She is the female equivalent of the successful businessman Deloney's novels describe; but she is no more free from patriarchal constraints (her usual childlessness strongly emphasizes this point) than Lodge's Rosalynd. Both kinds of idealizations, deriving from romance and bourgeois traditions, seem to reflect a desire to obliterate cultural uncertainties about the status of women. They provide a well-contained way of giving women power without giving them anything at all. Only Long Meg lives the completely idealized, self-determining life, and by so doing loses her reputation and the esteem of her society.

Riche's female characters are mired in oppression of various kinds, and their hardships are frequently stressed more emphatically than those of Riche's male figures. This imbalance may partially result from Riche's expressed desire to appeal to female readers, but it seems that it may also provide Riche's male readers with a sense of relief: if the problems of female characters are more graphic than those of male characters, if the power of men and fathers is repeatedly stressed (even while it is eventually defeated), then it must be possible for male readers to breathe more easily after reading the *Farewell*.

And yet, this positioning of the male is not unproblematic: the economic difficulties of women in the *Farewell* are not purely literary phenomena. For gentry aware of the declining wealth others of their class were experiencing and merchant-class readers aware of the exaggeration in Deloney's description of wealthy clothiers, there must have been an unconscious recognition of their experience through, for example, the mother of Lucilla. The instability of the lives of Riche's female characters corresponds to the uncertainty in the lives of Riche's readers, especially those who lacked immediate access to the means of power. The members of the growing merchant class and the declining gentry are in the position of Riche's female characters. They are Greenblatt's "threatening Other" opposing traditional English society. They are subject to what Lucilla's mother terms "euil Fortune" and "miserable necessitie" (95). Forcing female characters to suffer these difficulties allows male readers to define the nature and extent of their social troubles without having to admit their precariousness.

Unlike Lodge and Deloney, who perhaps chose a simpler route by trying to idealize female possibilities, Riche presents a bleaker view. He projects onto female characters the problems of his readers so that they may identify intimately (if they are female) or vicariously (if male) with his characters' political and economic insufficiencies. Female characters are made to bear the burden for all of Riche's readers.

5

Authorizing Landscapes

The Power of Place

THE PROJECTION of male anxieties and insecurities onto female characters is only one of several nonstructural methods by which the writers of Elizabethan novelistic discourse distance themselves from representations of the "threatening Other" embedded in their culture. Like the incorporation of foreign materials and poetry into the prose, the depiction of the female contributes to the ability of these writers to establish the authority of their genre. Similarly, the manipulation of descriptive language within novelistic discourse also enables Elizabethan pamphleteers to further establish their texts as literary works able to critique English culture. Discussion of description is particularly important in recovering what might be called a "fairer" critical representation of them. Some of the more typical arguments used to justify the widespread devaluation of Elizabethan novelistic discourse focus on its lack of specific detail, its generic plots and characters, and its generalized sense of place. One of the classic arguments of this type is E. M. Forster's brief dismissal in *Aspects of the Novel.* Early in his study Forster admits that Thomas Deloney does not differ "fundamentally" from modern novelists of equal quality, but he says that "the Elizabethan humorist picks up his victim in a different way from the modern, raises his laughs by other tricks." The novelist Deloney becomes a "humorist" and so disposable from a discussion of the novel that, with its emphasis on "flat" and "round" characters, seems designed in part to exclude Deloney and his contemporaries from the class of novelists.[1]

Frederick R. Karl's *The Eighteenth-Century Novel* provides another example of the centrality of description to assessments of novelistic discourse. Karl's differentiation between Elizabethan fiction and the modern novel similarly depends upon the notion of realism implicit in Forster's argument. Karl focuses on "eighteenth-century literary realism," roughly analogous to what Ian Watt terms "formal realism," as a means of defining the novel's genre; he even develops a fifteen-point checklist of characteristics typical of "novels" or "modern fiction." Of Karl's criteria, two are relevant here: first, he insists on the presentation of "man in his true physical setting, man who must be fed, clothed and sheltered"; and secondly, he finds essential the "use of denotative language aimed at communicating qualities that all men share—sense of touch, color, temperature, etc.—without regard for *how* they come to feel these sensations."[2]

Although I find Karl's general argument on the subversive nature of the novel useful, his emphasis on descriptive realism as an essential quality of the novel serves to erase Elizabethan novelistic discourse from the body of fiction worth serious scholarly consideration. Such dismissive arguments about Elizabethan novelistic discourse miss the point. They resist such arguments as Bakhtin's, which emphasize the function of novelistic texts within a given culture, and instead insist too literally that what Forster calls the "other tricks" that drive early fiction are wholly unrelated to more recent techniques. They categorize literature by its surface features and not by its role within the culture of its original readers. The uses of description in Elizabethan novelistic discourse, for instance, should not be evaluated by twentieth-century desires for encyclopedic detail, but perhaps instead in relation to Samuel Johnson's famous statement in *Rasselas* about the descriptive responsibilities of the writer:

> The business of the poet [or prose writer] . . . is to examine not the individual but the species; to remark general properties and large appearances: he does not number the streaks

of the tulip, or describe the different shades in the verdure of the forest. He is to exhibit in his portraits of nature such prominent and striking features, as recall the original to every mind; and must neglect minuter discriminations, which one may have remarked and another have neglected, for those characteristics which are alike obvious to vigilance and carelessness.[3]

It is these "prominent and striking features" that Elizabethan novelistic discourse stresses, except in certain instances in which more specific details promote well-defined ends, ends that revolve around attempts of the characters within the texts to authorize themselves, the class to which they belong, and the appropriateness of actions they desire to take.

The focus in this discussion will be primarily on descriptions of landscape and setting, since it is in large part the distinction between what Karl calls the representation of "man in his true physical setting, man who must be fed, clothed, and sheltered," and the generalizations of setting and character typical of romance that has worked to undermine the status of Elizabethan novelistic discourse. The tendency toward what Tzvetan Todorov calls a-psychological narratives, that is, toward narratives in which "action is important in itself" and not in relation to a specific aspect of a character's personality,[4] makes detailed descriptions of setting problematic within these texts. As locations to be sensually imagined, the settings are not always fundamentally important. Nonetheless, while such descriptions may not always elucidate character, they do define characters' cultural possibilities. The means by which the pamphleteers describe their locations represent the limits of the characters' socioeconomic positions—and the writers' relation to the ideologies of their culture.

The writers of criminal literature provided detailed descriptions of what they asked their readers to believe were attributes of England's criminal class (their language, their methods, and, in Harmon's case, their names) in an attempt to establish themselves as authorities on both their subject matter and their genre. Writers who made less of a claim to historical accuracy, or realism, similarly use specific detail to increase their credibility. Descriptions of setting allow these writers to increase their textual authority while exploiting that advantage to critique prevailing ideologies. Nicholas Breton's *The Miseries of Mavillia* (1597) and Barnabe Riche's "Fineo and Fiamma" provide two prominent examples of texts that manipulate descriptions of setting and location to analyze their readers' social position.

These two texts do not provide landscapes that could be termed "realistic" by the definitions Karl or Ian Watt use; instead, their settings, like those of most texts within their genre, are more frequently generalized. The Athens and Naples of *Euphues,* the estate of *The Adventures of Master F.J.,* and the undescribed Bohemia of *Pandosto* create the more dominant response to the nature of description and landscape in Elizabethan novelistic discourse. The long-standing distinction between "the country" and "the city," which Raymond Williams so thoroughly traced in English literature, also contributes to modes of description in Elizabethan novelistic discourse: the primitive communism Williams finds in sixteenth- and seventeenth-century literature, which stressed the ideal of the communal ownership of all goods and devalued individual possessions, lies behind the attitudes toward description expressed in much of the period's literature.[5]

I

Nicholas Breton's *The Miseries of Mavillia* uses a much greater degree of physical description to explore the limits of power and status than does Riche's "Fineo and Fiamma." In addition to descriptive strategies, the narrative techniques Breton employs—primarily the use of a first-person, female narrator and the depiction of formal landscapes and detailed descriptions of nature—challenge the reader to disengage completely the teller of the tale from its author and to accept the text as displaying a greater degree of "realism" (in the sense Karl or Watt use) than Elizabethan novelistic discourse typically employs.[6] This text becomes disinaugurated from the voice of Breton and so forces the reader to accept the text as a fictional work.

The Miseries of Mavillia, set "[i]n the troublesome time of a king unnamed, in a countrie too well knowne" (36), is divided into five chapters, or "miseries," in which Mavillia describes her life from early childhood until her death. Having been orphaned by war, Mavillia experiences a series of adventures including being cared for by a laundress who accompanies the invading army (whom Mavillia resents because, among other reasons, she makes Mavillia read too much), being sent with "two or three gallant gentlemen" and a young page to her uncle's house "in the countrey" (38), and being beseiged on this journey by highwaymen who murder all the travelers except Mavillia and her page. The two are eventually sheltered by an elderly couple and their daughter, but not before the page has accidentally shot himself, lamented the dangers of their desolation, killed a wild boar, and been wounded again. Very shortly after their rescue, the page dies. Mavillia's money is stolen by the couple, who treat her as a servant, and she is eventually wrongly accused of having stolen their money. Her innocence is at length revealed; she is restored to her socioeconomic position; and two suitors vie for her hand in marriage. Mavillia chooses the younger of the two men (their most distinguishing feature being their age), whereupon the older suitor revenges his rejection by biting off Mavillia's nose. Her husband remains true to her despite her disfigurement, and she spends "a wearie life" (51) with him. Years later, her husband slays the old suitor, but not before he is mortally wounded. Mavillia ends her tale by essentially narrating not only her husband's death but her own as well:

> Now I beeing great with childe, fell into a traunce, and recovered againe, I fell to dressing of his wounds, which bleeding sore, and he fainting, I was in no good case to behold. Let this suffice, hitherto I have written the tragicall discourse of my unhappy life. Now going to my husband, to see how he fares, [I saw] that he [was] left speechlesse,

[and I am] so weake my selfe, as that mine eyes doo faile me. In hope to goe to God, I bid you all farweell. (51)

Nature plays its largest role during Mavillia's voyage through the forest, where descriptions of the landscape emphasize Mavillia's helplessness, but formal descriptions of landscape occur twice in the text at points when the reader is encouraged to see Mavillia as trying to retain some control over her position in the narrative's rather frightening world. The decision to send her to her uncle occurs while Mavillia and the army's commanding captain walk in a garden, as does her decision to marry the younger suitor.

Neither garden is described—one garden is apparently the same as any other—but it is significant that these extremely important decisions are both made in gardens and that such settings are represented in no other parts of the narrative. This very formal landscape evokes the pastoral world that insulates characters in, for example, Boccaccio's *Decameron*. It provides a means of asserting some knowledge and understanding of nature by individuals who have some protection from its extremities. Allowing rational decisions and conscious choices to be made in these formal settings aligns Mavillia with aristocratic interpretations of nature that desire to assert control over it and over those individuals who have a less mediated experience of it—an experience of nature such as we see in what may be termed the story's passages of "realistic" natural description.[7]

We only catch a glimpse of the first "symbolic" landscape. Within the first paragraph of the second misery Mavillia reports: "one day in the morning, walking about a garden, he [the captain] called me to him, and there used this speech unto me" (38). Thereupon follows the captain's lengthy rationale for dispatching Mavillia to her uncle. She welcomes his decision beause she worries that left where she is she may either fall prey to vanity or "might be offered some villanie" (38). This first garden is not mentioned again. The second garden Breton depicts is the location of the adult Mavillia's contemplation of marriage and the site where she accepts the proposal of the younger suitor. There, too, she meets her older suitor, but finding him unpleasant, she quickly leads him out of the garden. She tells her readers: "To be short, I could not away with his [the old suitor's] stale jestes, and therefore making little answere to his propositions, I came out of the garden into the parler" (49). What seems significant in this case is the move to the "parler" when the garden ceases to be a location that insulates Mavillia.

There is evidence elsewhere in the text of the protective, nurturing nature of formal gardens. After the young Mavillia and her page have discovered the elderly couple's farmhouse, and the boy's wounds have been dressed, the old woman offers Mavillia some time in a garden to collect herself: "Will you go a little into the garden and gather a flower?" (40). Mavillia rejects her hostess's suggestion, choosing instead to remain near the page. The garden in *Mavillia* is a protective place: the presence of the old woman about to steal Mavillia's money prevents her entrance into it, just as the intrusion of the nose-biting old suitor causes a speedy exit from the later garden. The physical protection and insulation that gardens provide is also paralleled by a kind of "logical insulation" within them. In the early garden, for instance, the captain feels the need to make a lengthy defense of his decision to send Mavillia through an apparently unsafe land with a very small entourage, and the later garden is the site of Mavillia's equally lengthy ruminations on the nature of love.

The illusion that these gardens provide—that reason or individual behavior controls one's fate—is at odds with the picture created elsewhere in the text, and it differs most significantly from the description of the events that occur in the text's forest. There the powerlessness of the individual—and especially the orphaned aristocratic girl accustomed to a mediated experience of nature—is demonstrated. As with the references to gardens, the woods themselves are not described except in relation to their role in the plot, yet they play such an important role that we learn a great deal about them. The woods first make an appearance as the place from which Mavillia's attackers come: "suddainly, at unawares," she reports, "there issued out of a woodde a horseman or two, verie well appointed, who, drawing somewhat neare us, began to charge uppon us" (38). From this generalized introduction, nature becomes particularized to an extreme degree. For example, when Mavillia asks the page how they will be able to start a fire, he responds: "Oh, mistresse, the fire-locke of my pistoll, my match and a little powder in my flaske, and light my match; and then a fewe rotten stickes out of the hedge, and a few of these drie sedges, oh, they will burne roundly" (38). Later, after the page has accidentally shot himself in the thigh, elements of nature become even more thoroughly described. Mavillia stanches the bleeding by drying some of the boy's blood in the sun, then she grinds it into a powder and sprinkles it into the wound. The page requests further treatment: he asks her to find "Planten" leaves, which he tells her grow "neare the grounde" (39), because these leaves have "great strings" in them that may be used to close the wound and keep it clean. She rejects this idea because she has already found "wilde isope" (39), the medicinal properties of which her foster mother, the laundress, had taught her. These examples show the greatest degree to which aspects of the forest become particularized, but they are not the only instances in which detailed physical description appears. In this same location the two characters encounter a fox carrying a dead lamb and, later, the wild boar who mortally wounds the page. These details combine with the particularized description of the plantain and its uses to make the woods seriously threatening.

The forest produces the murderers who begin Mavillia's second set of troubles and the boar that wounds the page, and it affords him with the opportunity to shoot himself in the thigh. The elderly couple who rescue and then rob the pair live in that forest, adding to the contrast with the gardens that it provides. The forest, unlike the formal gardens in *Mavillia,* resists attempts at control by any instruments of societal law or rational thought: the woods act to equate graphically nature and un-reason. Mavillia and her page may use reason to promote their survival in the forest—they can discuss the best means for stopping bleeding or how to trap food, but their arguments and logical discussions are not focused on how to act but on how to react to the circumstances of their isolation. They do not reason, like the captain in the garden, about how to prevent problems from occurring; instead, their behavior is purely reactive.

There is one telling exception. Immediately following their ambush, Mavillia and the page view their murdered companions and realize that salvation from complete desolation lies in removing whatever money is in the corpses' pockets, but Mavillia cannot bring herself to touch the bodies.

> How shall I doo? a hungry stomack will call for meate, meate will not be had without money, money is none heere, except with the dead souldiours: and alas! my heart will not serve mee to rifle a carkasse; but see what is use? The page is in theyr pockettes, hee is filching for crownes. But come away, boye; alas! what good will money doo, where there is no meate to get? (38)

Money, in this passage, becomes the most important element in the forest world: had the boy not stolen from the corpses, the elderly couple would have had nothing to steal, and Mavillia's miseries would have been entirely different. What becomes lamented in the text as the vicissitudes of Fate are actually the result of economic troubles. It becomes clear that, regardless of the emphasis the narrative places on locations within the text, it is the presence of money and Mavillia's relatively high socioeconomic position that cause her travails. The description of setting reinforces the universality of the importance of economic standing and the interrelation between social position and economic strength. The page encourages Mavillia to hope that "God will send us some odde pesaunt or other" (38) willing to sell them bread and cheese. The boy seems convinced that urban rules—or, at least, the rules of a city at peace, which have established that money buys what those who have it want—will still apply in the natural world of "Planten" and "wilde isope." Unfortunately, the laws of a society that produces insulating gardens in which characters can stroll and exercise their logical powers do not function in the woods. Money remains crucially significant, but the social laws governing the deferential behavior on which the page and Mavillia depend do not.

Even under the best circumstances, reason and the rules of monied society do not hold in this world: Mavillia's wealthy family and the society that created it fall prey to attack in the fourth paragraph of the text, and they remain under siege throughout it. The formal garden protects characters from the uncertainties to which their economic loss subjects them. These gardens remain generic and undescribed because of the limited exposure characters have to such oases: Mavillia cannot describe the gardens in detail because she has not spent much time in them; when she gains access to them, her concentration must be focused on plots and plans to keep her protected from "villanie."

The realistic particularity of the forest provides the antithesis to the formal, symbolic garden. Breton is able to allow Mavillia to provide detailed descriptions of how to cope with the woods because she has spent considerable time in places not subject to economic and social hierarchies, and because while exposed to natural forces there is no time to describe anything unrelated to survival. Seen in this light, Mavillia's recollection of the healing properties of "wilde isope" should not surprise us. What should surprise us, if anything can by the time we reach the end of her narrative, is that she feels gardens should provide her with any protection at all. As the intrusion of the old suitor shows her—and us—they do not.

II

While Breton's description of settings permits him to establish problematic distinctions between societal and physical realms, Riche's "Fineo and Fiamma" generally provides little description of the characters, settings, and events it relates. Nonetheless, it is not true that Riche's use of physical description is "either perfunctory or [provides] merely inventories of objects," as Lennard J. Davis—demonstrating general agreement with Karl—defines "pre-novelistic description."[8] Elaborating on his source in Giraldi Cinthio's *Hecatommithi,* Riche's use of description in the text is hardly perfunctory. Instead, he employs descriptions of location and physical objects in emphatic ways to explore kinds of governmental structures and approaches to political power. This exploration provides alternatives to prevailing definitions of societal constraints and formations. Riche's text presents two definitions of social control and then, by means of his use of setting, dismantles that opposition by creating a third locale that refuses to be defined by either oppositional term. This border location creates a site, somewhat like *Mavillia*'s forest, where the implications of societal definitions can be explored and where societal constructions such as law and language can be interrogated.

"Fineo and Fiamma," the fourth narrative in the *Farewell,* is a Heliodoran romance describing the adventures of two young, Italian lovers who eventually overcome the opposition of the woman's family and enslavement in Tunis to marry and, presumably, live happily ever after. Riche himself summarizes the novella in its argument, saying that it contains

> The harde aduenture of *Fineo,* with his beloued *Fiamma,* who after sondrie conflictes of Fortune, were in the ende solde as slaues to the Kyng of *Tunise,* who seying their perfecte loue caused them to be Maried, and after honouryng theim with sondrie presentes, sent them home to [Genoa], whereby their Parentes and freendes, thei were ioyfully receiued. (106)

Riche generalizes and, as is typical of his arguments, elides many of the text's important points: the illegal duel between Fineo and Fiamma's brother that results in Fineo's being cast adrift, Fiamma's attempt to duplicate the death she imagines her lover has endured, Fineo's capture by a frigate of Moorish pirates, Fiamma's betrayal by the Moor whose aid she had enlisted, *her* capture by a second frigate of pirates, and the capture of the second frigate by the first. These are Riche's "sondrie conflictes." Once in Tunis, Fiamma becomes a member of the king's harem, which is so large that Fiamma's virginity remains unthreatened for more than a year, providing enough time for relatives to arrive from Italy, make plans to rescue the lovers, return to Italy, and sail again to Tunis to effect their release. Within about twelve hours of their departure from Tunis, a storm drives their ship back toward shore and they are recaptured. At this point, as the argument states, the king sees their love, releases them, and gives them, among other gifts, a large ruby wedding ring.

Riche creates two societies in this narrative and expends considerable energy to demonstrate their conformity and responsiveness to precepts of law and language. The cities of Genoa and Tunis are equally developed, and both are described not in terms of houses, terrain, streets, and marketplaces, but almost exclusively in terms of their laws. In Genoa we learn of a law that prohibits men from carrying weapons and fighting in the streets, a law similar to one in the Rome of Nashe's *The Unfortunate Traveller,* a law that Fiamma's brother plans to defy; we also learn, however, of the specific exemption from the law that governs the men's actions.

> For although there were at that tyme a very straight lawe in the Citie, that no manne should weare his sworde, and paine of death appointed for him that should hurte any man with any weapon: Yet bothe these gentlemen weare their swordes, for that thei bothe had charge of souldiers, that laye then in garrison for defence of the Citie. (107)

Fiamma's brother subsequently provokes a sword fight and is slightly injured. Fineo's death sentence is commuted to his abandonment at sea because he is "verie well freended, and suppored by many principall gentlemen of the citie" (108). In other words, what Riche presents in this novella is a society governed by laws, explicitly expressed in language, that first seem inapplicable to the characters and then not absolute: Genoa is a society in which legal discourse dominates behavior, but in which this law—because it is constructed of language—can be confused and manipulated by other linguistic acts. Law is only as absolute as language. A change in language changes the law.[9]

Riche's Tunis presents a culture with a similar reliance on law, but a law that has a different foundation and is manipulated by different means. In Tunis, the most important law pertains to the "Cube," the king's harem, and to the king's treatment of his concubines:

> The maner [and] custome of the Kyng was, to cause his [concu]bines to come vnto him, and to lye with them by order, [as] thei had been bought or come to his handes: By reason of [w]hiche custome, for that there were very many bought before [t]he commyng thether of *Fiamma*, there was alreadie a whole [ye]are and a halfe welnie paste after her sale, and yet her turne [w]as not come to be called for. (113)

In this instance, the emphasis is on "maner [and] custome," but, as the strict adherence to this tradition shows, it possesses the force of law. In Tunis, however, the force of law is not as easily subverted as it is in Genoa, partly because here Riche's protagonists are not part of the aristocratic elite. Also, however, subversion is less possible because Riche's portrayal of their isolation reflects the common tendency in the period to depict African and Middle Eastern cultures as barbaric and uncivilized—not as "cultures" at all and, therefore, not equally susceptible to the sophisticated inducements of language and, in fact, not possessing the capacity for logical, rational argument.[10] Part of the problem, too, arises from difficulties with the nature of language that can be used in Genoa to deconstruct legal meaning and action. In Tunis, law is not linguistic; it is the product of habitual action, of "custome," and, therefore, it does not respond to language. It can only be undone by other habitual action (hence the need for the rescuers to come twice to Tunis). The lovers cannot talk their way out of their enslavement and Fiamma's eventual rape, as Fiamma's occasional references to her inability to speak well or understand fully her captors' language emphasize. It takes the action of their escape, the storm at sea that keeps them near shore, and the silent tears of Fiamma to effect their release. In other words, only action—and action that focuses on a third locale, the sea—allows for subversion of the law.

Even when language does figure prominently in the narrative, its value is dwarfed by the description of physical action. Fineo manages to convey to Fiamma a letter explaining an escape plan hidden in a purse that his relatives (posing as Italian traders) have presented to her while distributing gifts to the king's concubines.

> The brother of *Fineo* presented *Fiamma* emong the reste, with a very faire Purse richely embrodered with golde and Pearle, in the whiche there was enclosed a letter, written by *Fineo*, by the contentes whereof she might vnderstande at large, al that whiche he did wishe and would haue her doe, to make their escape together, and to ridde them selues out of that thraldom and captiuitie. (115)

Here it is action, the giving of the purse, that allows the law to be subverted: language is, in this case, enclosed inside action. What is more significant about this passage is, first, that action must precede language and second, the description of the purse. Its gold and pearl embroidery are the most specific physical details we receive about any character, setting, or object in "Fineo and Fiamma," and the details emphasize the strength of Tunisian law and the difficulties that surround a reliance on language in Eastern surroundings. The exchange of the purse signals the overt beginning of the overthrow of both Genoan and Tunisian law, but that process is fundamentally begun, as well as ended, by the action of the sea.

The sea provides a landscape without hegemony or ownership: neither Genoa nor Tunis controls it. Both countries attempt to impose their law upon the sea (during the Genoese attempt to execute Fineo via the sea or, for example, the king of Tunis's ocean pursuit of the escaping lovers), but neither is effective (Fineo is rescued and the storm preempts the chase). The only social order presented on the sea consists of the two frigates of pirates who separately capture Fineo and Fiamma and then battle for control of the prisoners. An additional attempt to control events or characters at sea is made by Fiamma's servant, who, like the pirates, is a Moor.

When Fiamma attempts to cast herself adrift, she enlists the aid of one of her father's Moorish slaves, who is to row her down the coast from Genoa, where he will be awarded his freedom. She will then cast herself out to sea. The Moor agrees, but secretly plans to guide her boat to Tunis and sell her into slavery. He is mortally wounded when the frigate of Moors captures them. After he dies, the narrative tells us that "he hauyng thought by treacherie, and breakyng of his faithe, to make greate gaine, loste bothe his life and all that, whiche he had gotten of the vnaduised, and euill counselled yong gentlewoman" (112). Again, it is Genoese language—"evil counsel"—that has caused Fiamma's problems. The Moor's death also results from language: he breaks "his faithe." His actions do not correspond to his words and under Genoese law, promises—language—can only be broken by other acts of language, not by physical action, no matter how murderous those actions may be. The sea, in other words, recognizes duplicitous language and punishes it in a way Italian society does not.

As we know from the narrative's argument, there is a twist. Before the slave dies, he reveals to Fiamma's new captors her aristocratic background, explains his own plan to sell her in Tunis, and convinces them to fulfill his intention. At sea, his language effects the action he desired: language holds as law when the Italian characters are involved, but it is altered by action. The slave's plan is fulfilled, but not by him. His language governs the treatment of Fiamma but prevents his action, and the boundaries between language and action become blurred. The slave is freed on the sea from adherence to a language-based law, but that freedom to act also coexists with a possibility that action-based law, the capture by the frigate, will supersede and contradict it. The liberation the sea allows creates a contradictory definition of law or control: the slave's language authorizes another character's actions while he himself is not permitted to act.

The sea presents similarly contradictory definitions for other characters as well. Fineo and Fiamma greet the pirates as rescuers, although the pirates view themselves differently; the first Italian delegation is brought to Tunis as merchants, not as saviors, and they are not allowed to do more to aid the lovers during that first trip than to carry letters back to Fineo's family;[11] the escaping Italians are permitted to send back one of their company in a small boat before the wind returns the ship to Tunis, and that individual is able to reach Genoa despite the storm. In this final instance, the sea provides an escape not so that the character can return with Italian reinforcements, but so he can tell the story of the escape attempt to Fineo's father: the action-based law of Tunis has been transformed into the Italian language-based law. The sea adheres to neither definition of law: language is not binding on its speakers, nor is action—as of the storm—universally binding. The fulfillment of the Moor's words subverts language on the sea. Although he dies, he has formulated the plan that violates his promise to Fiamma. Language is further subverted by the pirates who deliver Fiamma to the king of Tunis. They are only able to sell Fiamma because of their belief in their right to board and capture ships they encounter (what we might call piratical law). The frigate that captures Fineo adheres to this same piratical code—a law of action that does not explicitly concern itself with vindication on the grounds of "custome" and which does not produce a hegemonic society. The pirates follow a law that does not restrain free action to a ruling individual or group: there is no central authority that produces laws which must be followed, nor is there a sense that the frigate which on one occasion fights more effectively will continue to do so. The pirate band that captured Fiamma could just as easily have defeated Fineo's captors.

This piratical law that operates on the sea seems based on separate, unconnected acts of strength, Fortune, and the whims of nature. Language-based law and tradition-based law are shown to be inefficient and unreliable at sea. In this location, piratical strength and Fortune rule, and, ultimately, suggest more reliable (if less comforting) models of power and authority. Language, Italian society shows us, is limited as the basis for a legal system because language itself provides an ever-present threat; moreover, it must depend upon a form of natural justice (in the casting adrift of Fineo) to complete its intentions. Tradition-based law leads to the threat of rape and the need for deceit: the attempt in Tunis to reassert the power of language must, after all, be hidden in a purse designed as a gift to placate the concubines and make them tolerant of their enslavement and rape. And this image, remember, is described in more detail than any other in the entire novella.

Riche's conclusion seems, however, to try to reject the definitions of power the sea provides. It pushes the lovers back to Tunis, where their love is made clear to the king through "the teares of *Fiamma* and the onelie name of Loue" (118). In other words, as the text comes to a close, Riche tries to combine the action-based law (her tears) with language-based law ("the onelie name of Loue"). Tunisian law prompts the king to release them and support their marriage. He confirms his endorsement of their union by taking "from his owne finger a merueilous faire and precious Rubie" (117), the only object besides the purse specifically described by the narrative, and presenting it as a wedding ring for Fiamma. This action removes the lovers from subjection to the law of the sea and reinserts them into the Tunisian system. It is true that the combination of action—the giving of the ring— and the king's prior verbal endorsement of the marriage suggests a certain degree of change in Tunisian legal standards, but there is no indication that the king's action will have any broader application within his realm: he will continue to maintain his customary practices with his concubines.

The minor alteration in Tunisian law is not paralleled by any transformation of Genoese law. The lovers' homecoming to Italy reinstalls them into a society ruled by language. Since the two are already married, the family of Fiamma no longer protests the match. Neither society reevaluates its mode of power as a result of the incident, and the two lovers show no sign of having any power to reform Genoese society. The two societies, quietly linked at the beginning of the text by subtle references to the pride the editor calls "characteristic of the Genoese" (282), are overtly linked at the story's close by their mutual endorsement of the marriage. The paradigms of power the sea presented are forgotten by the narrative. The characters quickly sail away from the slim chance for change Tunis provided. Eerily, the sea helps the king of Tunis temporarily revise his legal system, and it then removes the Italians from the land where this new system might just be evolving—or could have evolved had the lovers, the products of the sea-changed system, remained.[12]

Instead, the sea remains a border between laws of language and laws of tradition: a place where the two laws mix and negate each other. It is a place where both lose force, and the only semblance of a functioning society it allows is that of the non-European pirates who must continually create power and authority during each individual encounter. The only response of Europeans to this legal system is silence and gesture. When Fineo and Fiamma realize that they have been captured by the same frigate, for example, they do not speak or conspire to act. Instead, *"Fineo* made figu[r]es to *Fiamma,* that in nowise she should take knowledge, or acquaintaunce of hym, and accordyngly she dissembled and made no shewe, but as one had neuer seen hym" (112). Only "figures," not language, only the reluctance to act overtly, not action itself, sustain Europeans on the sea. And it does work. Fineo and Fiamma have no trouble understanding each other, and their behavior does allow them to remain together in Tunis.

Although we know little about the physical appearance of the Tunis the lovers eventually leave, the Genoa to which they return, or the sea that subverts the laws that govern them, we know all we need to know: description of these settings is confined to description of law because it is the nature of law and societal controls that is explored in "Fineo and Fiamma." Physical description in this text is restricted to two objects—the purse and the ring—emblematic of the nature and strength of those laws.

Rather than faulting Riche for not providing a "realistic" setting, we should recognize that he has created a world that responds to his concerns about economic and class status. By translating and adapting Giraldi Cinthio's tale, Riche has explored the implications of membership in cultures ruled by legal discourse, by tradition, and by dependence upon physical force instead of either mode of cultural control. He further questions the value of status without wealth and the linkages between hereditary and economic power. The societal definitions he confronts force his readers to assess their own alliances within English culture and to interrogate the web of laws and traditions present within the evolving Elizabethan world. The system of cultures Riche establishes in "Fineo and Fiamma" may cause his readers to empathize with Tunisian culture, if they resent the decline of feudal tradition, and such a moment of recognition should subvert those traditional impulses. Should his readers empathize with the Genoese government, they must accept responsibility for the punishment of the lovers, their capture, and the knowledge that their laws were arbitrarily manipulated by political influence. Should readers empathize with the title characters of the narrative, as the text seems to encourage, they must accept their powerlessness and their subjection to arbitrary, malleable traditions and legalistic formality.

Riche's description, although limited to very specific instances and kinds of detail, provides his readers with representations of their culture in conflict. As they work their way through Riche's narrative they must continually reevaluate their ideological position. As they engage in that process, they authorize Riche's text and his role as author: they grant to him and his work the ability to guide them through their self-analysis. By the conclusion of the narrative, however, they must confront Riche's failure to create for them a stable position either within the text or within their world.

III

The settings in which social and economic hierarchies operate are described more explicitly in Breton's *The Miseries of Mavillia* than they are in Riche's "Fineo and Fiamma." Breton's use of physical detail contributes greatly to the more detailed exploration of the limits of power and status his text entails. Riche confines his use of physical description to very specific objects central to his narrative's plot and emphasizes instead the detailed analysis of the laws governing the locations to provide the context for his critique of the constraints placed upon his readers. Breton stresses physical description more strongly in order to explore the limitations of power to which the monied classes were subject; Riche provides his readers with isolated descriptive details in his quest to undermine the socially constructed hierarchies that surround and define his characters.

Neither of these texts consistently details Johnson's "streaks of the tulip." Instead, both Breton and Riche determine the aspects of society and the social limitations they are determined to emphasize and use description to establish the focus of their social commentary. The helplessness of Mavillia and the troubles of Fineo and Fiamma are the result of societal expectations dependent upon their class status and their inability to fulfill society's demands. Fineo and Fiamma choose to contract a prohibited marriage. Mavillia refuses to accept both that her parents' death has altered her economic and social status and that her gender makes it extremely difficult for her to reclaim her social position. Significant, too, especially in Riche's *Farewell,* is that moments of description occur when characters are removed from their conventional social world (hence, the purse and the ring are both described in the context of Tunis). In the presence of cultural Otherness, Elizabethan novelistic discourse is compelled to describe its limits, as well as those of its authors and readers.

6

Constructing the Alien, Authorizing the Self

—

THE DESCRIPTION of place in Elizabethan novelistic discourse is key to the texts' function because it creates a ground against which writers and readers can position themselves and their relation to the culture they simultaneously construct and are constructed by. Part of what becomes crucial to the depiction of place within these narratives is the relation that is established between English and foreign cultures that may be figured as generally as the "countrie too well knowne" of Breton's *Mavillia*, the "America" of Lodge's *Margarite*, or the Arcadia of Sidney's romance. Place becomes an even more significant metaphor within Elizabethan novelistic discourse when it confronts non-European characters or cultures through which writers and readers may establish the limits of their own identity and their expectations for their social and economic class. It also provides the writers of these texts with a way to test and refine their own sense of the collective identity of their readers without overtly threatening their readers' sense of definition by implicating the culture to which they and their readers belong. Hiding behind the claim that they are simply reproducing characters and settings from their source material, writers of Elizabethan novelistic discourse are able to challenge their readers' expectations of themselves and their culture. The ability of literary texts to permit such exploration is not new to the Renaissance. Kittay and Godzich observe its presence within medieval narratives, most notably *Song of Roland,* and comment that: "It is indeed in these representations of otherness that the imaginary gives us a glimpse of the society's self-understanding as it makes explicit the boundaries of what it will consider an 'unthinkable,' although formulatable, alternative to itself."[1]

Discussion of the relationship of foreign sources to these texts has already enabled us to glimpse the advantages derived from employing foreign characters and distant geographic locations. Although it would be naive to assume that readers fully ascribed to these texts the qualities popularly tied to their foreign locations and sources of origin, it would also be naive to assume that Elizabethan readers completely ignored popular perceptions of specific geographic locales: popular perceptions of Eastern cultures functioned as inescapable "baggage" carried by Elizabethan readers. Sixteenth-century views of non-European cultures as alien to the English experience provided writers of Elizabethan novelistic discourse with sites more removed from their readers' experience, sites that permitted a more highly problematized discussion of the oppositions between reader and society, between collective self and public Other.

Barnabe Riche's *Farewell* provides several examples of ways in which Eastern cultures are manipulated in these texts to further a sense of authority and self-definition in its readers, but it is not the only text to raise these issues. Other Elizabethen prose narratives that use the East as a source of settings or characters seem to show more conformity to stereotypes of Turks—and their equivalents, Moors and Jews—as figures who reveal their intrinsic evil and godless barbarism. A brief look at four examples, Painter's "A Cruell Facte of Soltan Solyman" and "The Kinge of Marrocco," Munday's *Zelauto,* and Nashe's *The Unfortunate Traveller,* should reveal different ways in which Eastern characters are used to affirm and authorize their writers' and readers' ideological identity. The conventional ways in which these texts depict non-European characters and settings will provide a context in which to read Riche's more complex treatment of the East. In Riche's *Farewell,* the most prevalent Other presented to the reader is "the Turke." References to the Ottoman Empire generally or to "the

Turke" figure significantly in three of Riche's tales: "Sappho Duke of Mantona," "Apolonius and Silla," and "Aramanthus borne a Leper." In addition, a fourth story, "Fineo and Fiamma," focuses heavily on Tunisians and Moors, and the text's conclusion was revised in 1606 to include references to "the Turke" and Constantinople.[2] The question to be addressed in the argument that follows is to what effect Elizabethan writers of novelistic prose used images of Eastern cultures, and, more specifically, what kinds of readings are authorized by Riche's use of Eastern characters and settings.

The work of Edward W. Said, especially the very influential *Orientalism,* has done a great deal to inform critical thinking about the representation of Eastern cultures in Western literature. His work has shown the extent to which Western views of oriental cultures have dehumanized and objectified those cultures; he has demonstrated ways in which Western cultures have appropriated Eastern cultures in order to reconstruct and control them. Western cultures have, Said makes plain, colonized the East culturally as well as politically. Said's argument focuses on the academic institution of oriental studies, but colonization of the East can be traced much further back within the history of Western culture and English literature, as can be seen in an analysis of Samuel Chew's *The Crescent and the Rose* (1937).[3]

Chew's work, which is still very useful, attempts to document the uses of Islamic history and culture in early modern England. His focus is not on misrepresentations of Eastern culture, but instead on borrowings from it by sixteenth- and seventeenth-century writers (especially dramatists); nonetheless, his analysis establishes that English writers selected and exaggerated certain aspects of Eastern cultures in order to create a sense of the East consonant with their own goals. For example, Chew cites the murders by Selim the Grim of his father, Beyazid (Bajazeth), and his brothers in the early sixteenth century as the events most central in fixing "in the imagination of Europe the impression of barbarous cruelty and ruthless determination as qualities of Ottoman emperors," a sense of the Ottomans necessary in order to portray them in literature as embodiments of godless evil. The

Battle of Lepanto (1571) was also significant in this regard since although the Turks were defeated, the magnitude of the conflict (about 30,000 soliders participated on each side) demonstrated the size and strength of the Ottoman Empire. The Elizabethan state itself authorized racism against the East when, in 1599 and 1601, Queen Elizabeth complained about the number of North African Moors in England and called for their transportation.[4]

The colonized sense of the East of which Chew provides ample evidence functioned as any form of racism does: it allowed the English to project their fears, insecurities, and doubts about their own internal Otherness—about their nation, their religion, and their economic status—onto a safe, dehumanized group. The added advantage of England's physical distance from the Ottoman Empire, and the empire's well-known military strength, added to the ease with which the English colonized the Turks: they could claim that the Turks' military strength justified their belief in Turkish barbarism, while the distance between the Ottoman Empire and England limited the real threat the Turks could pose. The incursion of the Turks into Hungary in the mid-sixteenth century and the Battle of Lepanto were the closest the Ottoman Empire came to becoming an actual political threat to the English, so the unreality of the Ottoman Empire helped make it an apt target for accumulated English fears. These anxieties were solidified in large part by prevailing English Protestant attitudes toward the threat the Ottomans posed to English Christianity. A brief excerpt from a prayer by John Foxe demonstrates the religious fears about the East in general and "the Turke" in particular:

> First, the *Turke* w[ith] his sword, what landes, nations, and countreyes, what empires, kingdomes, and prouinces with Cities innumerable hath he wonne, not from us, but from thee [God]: where thy name was wont to be inuocated, thy word preached, thy Sacramentes administred, there now reigneth barbarous *Mahumet*, w[ith] his filthy *Alcoran*. The florishing Churches in *Asia,* the learned Churches of *Grecia,* the manifold Churches in *Africa* which were wont to serue thee, now are gone from thee.... In all the kyngdomes of

Syria, Palestina, Arabia, Persia, in all *Armenia,* and the Empire of *Capadocia,* through the whole compasse of *Asia,* with *Ægypt,* and with *Africa* also (vnles amongest the farre *Æthiopians* some old steppes of Christianitie peraduenture yet do remayne) either els in all *Asia* and *Africa,* thy Church hath not one foote of free land, but all is turned either to infidelitie, or to captiuitie, what soeuer pertaineth to thee.... All *Thracia* with the Empire of *Constantinople,* all *Grecia, Epyrus, Illyricum,* and now of late all the kyngdome almost of *Hungaria,* with much of *Austria,* with lamentable slaughter of Christen bloud is wasted, and all become *Turkes.*[5]

Like Foxe's prayer, much Elizabethan novelistic discourse perpetuates to a certain extent the stereotype of "the Turke" as inhuman and cruelly barbarous, but Riche's treatment of the Ottoman Empire does not simply conform to that dominant view. In contrast to the version of the East that Chew finds prevalent in the period is the view presented in Francesco Guicciardini's *The History of Italy* and repeated in Geoffray Fenton's 1579 translation, *The Historie of Guicciardin.* Although Fenton does refer occasionally to the "cruell slaughter" of prisoners of war or to the bloody process of succession in the empire, Guicciardini and Fenton generally present unsensationalized accounts of the behavior of the Turkish Empire. Guicciardini especially seems capable of reducing bias against the Turks. Although he does occasionally use emotionally loaded language that segregates the Turks from the group of Christian princes, Guicciardini more frequently treats the Ottoman Empire as any other foreign power of which Italy must be wary. Guicciardini is even willing to praise the erudition and religious fervor of Beyazid. Fenton's translation is relatively faithful to Guicciardini's text, given the fact that Fenton knew no Italian and worked from Chomeday's French translation; and where he does elaborate on the text, it is usually to include additional *conciones* by historical figures or to engage in anti-Catholic propaganda.[6]

Fenton's text itself seems to downplay the Turks' role in it. For example, "The General Contents of Euery Booke through the whole Historie" mentions the Turks only in reference to Book 20, regardless of their importance in earlier sections of the history.[7] Since there were other views of the Turks available to Riche (and Fenton's translation of Guicciardini was popular enough to merit three editions between 1579 and 1616), we need to account for the ways in which Eastern characters and settings function in Riche's *Farewell* and the period's more typical narrative prose.

The four novellas of the *Farewell* in which Eastern or Turkish characters are prominent create a means through which European characters are able to define themselves. In the texts that dramatize the non-European characters, "the Turke" and the King of Tunis provide important complications to happy plot resolutions: complications that must be resolved in order to permit definitions of individuals and socioeconomic groups. As we have previously seen, the characters in these narratives struggle to reach a condition of stasis: their plots usually involve quests for union with family or a beloved, or both. In Riche's tales, the presence of "the Turke" or the King of Tunis helps these characters refine their search—the East permits Europeans to define or refine the limits of their goals and, ultimately, of their own identity.

Yet these characters are not simply blocking figures. Eastern characters function as simultaneously "other" and "self": they are both "us" and "them," and they function in this capacity because of the strength and power English culture ascribed to them. They possess monolithic military ability and an internal domestic strength that made them attractive for stereotypical representations and appropriate figures for Riche's more complex goals. As will become apparent through our discussion of "Aramanthus borne a Leper," Riche's Eastern characters are able to combine simultaneously much of what Elizabethan culture repelled as well as much of what it found attractive.

This formulation seems somewhat similar to Walter R. Davis's presentation in *Idea and Act in Elizabethan Fiction* of Elizabethan novelistic discourse as a forum in which the world of ideas comes into contact with and is tested by a world of experience. However, the "ideas" that these works test are concerns about the collective identity of the readership and the nature of artistic authority, and they deemphasize the role of "experience." In the novelistic texts in which Eastern cultures occur, the sense of collective identity is strengthened, modified, and developed in opposition to the sense of the "alien" presented. Writers of Elizabethan discourse present versions of the East generally and of the Turks in particular that allow them to explore different aspects of class definition and artistic authority. As a result, it is not surprising that the image of the Ottoman Empire and of Moors and Jews is more reflective of Elizabethan desires for the self and England than it is of the Eastern cultures themselves.

This conclusion, in light of Said's *Orientalism,* is not surprising, but it does not mean that Elizabethan views of the East were monolithic. Guicciardini's version of the East (in Fenton's translation) is wary but respectful, treating the Ottomans as a particularly powerful political force but not being unduly hostile to them. Thomas Newton's *A Notable Historie of the Saracens* (1575), on the other hand, calls itself a "historicall Discourse of Saracens, Turks, and other Reprobates."[8] Similarly, the period's novelistic discourse does not uniformly depict a single stereotype, as we shall see. Nashe's *The Unfortunate Traveller,* for instance, particularizes and ridicules Jews in a fashion much different from Riche's *Farewell.*

I

Two Painter novellas respond conventionally to the idea of the East. "A Cruell Facte of Soltan Solyman," a retelling of the murder of Suleiman's son, Mustapha, is included, the narrator reports, because "I would haue it continue in man's remembraunce thereby to renue the aunciente detestation, which we haue, and our Progenitors had against that horrible Termagant, and Persecutor of Chrystians."[9] The view of the Ottoman empire in this passage parallels that of Guicciardini's allusion to the natural hatred of Turk for Christian, but Painter's text seems interested in much more than simply provoking racial hatred. Painter's story places a great deal of emphasis on explaining the Ottoman system of government and its hierarchies. We learn, for instance, that a "Bascha (which we commonly call VVascha) is the lieutenant of a Prouince" who holds a three year term (3:395). We also learn of a noble rank called "Spahy ... [a term denoting] the first degree of honour, but it hath no discent of succession to the Posterity" (3:398). "Soltan Solyman" contains many additional examples: it seems that this narrative is also designed to teach its readers about the Turks so that they will possess the language necessary to continue to isolate "them" from "us." Providing the Ottoman names for dignitaries—frequently with their English equivalents ("Subasche, which worde so farre as I can vnderstande, may be referred to the Title of Baron" [3:398])—furnishes readers with the means to appropriate the East: Painter's text creates not just a simple tale of political murder, but also a piece of history that authorizes his readers to claim a degree of understanding about the East and its relation to English culture. Painter's tale also allows readers to define points of equivalence between Eastern culture and their own: as "subasche" and "baron" become linked, Eastern and Elizabethan culture are shown to share fundamental similarities. The correspondences Painter's strategy illustrates provide a means through which he may describe the Other present within his culture without directly confronting it. Providing his readers with this information allows them to define themselves as a superior group, a group knowledgeable about a culture they have never experienced.

In "The Kinge of Marrocco," on the other hand, "knowledge" is not provided. Instead, this text describes the love and duty that a subject owes his or her sovereign. The novella is set in Africa, in "the Land of Oran . . . wher the inhabitants (although the soyle be barbarous) lyue indifferent ciuilly, vsing great curtesie to Straungers, and largely departing their goodes to the poore, towards whom they be so earnestly bente, and louing, as for theyr Lyberality and pytiful almesse, they shame vs Christians" (3:418). Inserting the narrative into this setting transforms the East into a source of Western "shame." Painter implies that the inhabitants of this "barbarous" "soyle" are more courteous and respectful toward their monarch than the English. In tales of this kind (and we will see that Munday's *Zelauto* functions similarly) the East is presented as a source of resentment: it is a place shown to be in some ways an idealized version of England. The East becomes a place where romanticization may occur, where fantastic examples of patriotism may be realized. The "land of Oran" presents another form of the Turkish strength we will see more fully in Riche's "Aramanthus borne a Leper." In Riche's text, however, the projection onto the East of desires for military and political power is more fully and logically motivated than it is here: while Painter's story seems to support unilateral backing of the queen, can we posit as much faith in this position among his readership?

Anthony Munday's *Zelauto* (1580) also presents an idealized East—in this case Persia, the location of the text's entire second book.[10] In this section, which Scanlon likens to a "medieval sermon" the wandering heir to the Duchy of Naples saves the life of a woman (the niece of the soldan) condemned to die because of her Christianity. Munday emphasizes Persia's hostility toward Christianity, a hostility that extends to its visitors: Christian travelers may spend ten days within the city of Zebaia, but after that period they remain at "their owne peryll, in which tyme, the Hoste [of the Christians] must be sworn for [their] good vsage, and to see if that [they] keepe due and decent behauiour in his house" (66). Regardless of this description of a world hostile to Christian travelers (and Zelauto's host is ultimately executed for his guest's behavior), an idealized view of a Christian emerges from the episode.

Zelauto learns of the impending execution of the soldan's niece; moreover, he learns that the soldan has decreed that her life will be spared if any knight successfully challenges his champion. Zelauto is the only hope: for a Persian to volunteer and fail would lead to his own execution for religious treason. In this episode, Zelauto, who becomes idealized as a selfless Christian hero, reasons with himself after he hears of the woman's plight:

... if I lost my lyfe in defence of my faith, my Captayne Christe would purchase me the greater reward. Again, if the Lady were so constant, to abyde such mercilesse tormentes as her owne kyndred, and the residue of her enimies would wyllingly lay vpon her, and all for the zealous Christianitie which remayned in her vertuous brest: I should deseruedly reape a great reproche, if I could and would not seeke to mittigate her miseries. Therfore wholy committing the cause to Gods omnipotencie, and not accoumpting of my life, to set foorth his glorie: I enterprised the matter courragiously, in assured hope to foyle the enimie. And if that afterwarde my death by any meanes should be conspired: I would referre all to the wyll of the almightie. (77)

Perhaps seeing this speech in relation to idealized views of Christianity becomes less successful if it is read in the context of Foxe's *Acts and Monuments,* but the way in which Zelauto can continue to express these sentiments—even when facing the soldan and, later, when he is imprisoned for slaying the soldan's champion— seems to transform Zebaia into a place where Christian acts not possible in Munday's England can take place.[11]

This view of Munday's Persia as an idealized representation of England receives some support in an odd book by William Kittle, *Edward de Vere, 17th Earl of Oxford and Shakespeare.* In his discussion of connections between *Zelauto* and Oxford, the dedicatee of the work, Kittle identifies the soldan of Zebaia with Queen Elizabeth. His reasons seem to be that *Zelauto* includes a series of verses in praise of Elizabeth and that Zelauto's speech to the soldan would be a suitable speech to make to the Queen. He further identifies Zelauto with the Earl of Oxford and the niece of the soldan with Oxford's poetic muse. While Kittle's argument seems improbable, his desire to identify England with Munday's Persia is fascinating. He must allegorize the Christian woman into a muse (an interpretive act the text does not seem to authorize) in order to avoid accusing Elizabeth of executing Christians, but nonetheless this identification turns Munday's Persia into the simultaneously attractive and repulsive force it becomes in Riche's Turkey.[12] *Zelauto*'s East becomes identified with the impossibilities of pure Christian action and becomes engaged in an uncomfortable relationship between the reader and the soldan that is ultimately masochistic. The nobility of Zelauto is attractive: as readers we support his response to the impending execution, and yet on a more realistic level we cannot honestly believe we would respond similarly. Fortunately, he escapes from prison and is not executed for his actions, so Munday's readers are saved from making the final identification of ourselves as martyrs: we (and Zelauto) are permitted the pleasure of martyrdom without the fact of it.

Nashe's *The Unfortunate Traveller* presents a much more limited, but ultimately much more frightening, sense of the East. During its Roman episode Nashe presents isolated Jewish characters—representatives of the colonized group withdrawn from the writer's perception of their native land and inserted into European culture. Perhaps because Nashe's work is much more satirical than any of the fictions we have examined thus far, his Eastern characters are much more broadly defined. Nashe's Jews, Zadoch and Doctor Zacharie, appear in *The Unfortunate Traveller* after a lengthy discourse on the follies of travel, and they seem (at least in part) to demonstrate the dangers of foreign influences even while at home. Jack Wilton, seeking shelter from a rain shower in Rome, leans up against an unlocked cellar door and tumbles into Zadoch's house and the world of the Jews. The dangers of travel, of exposure to other cultures, need not only occur outside the West. Of course, this episode occurs in Rome, not England, but Jack identifies himself just prior to the Jewish episode as "a banisht exile" from England who has lived for several years in Italy as an "outlaw."[13] Italy becomes a kind of England for Jack, even while it operates as a very foreign Other. It is significant to note, too, that the list of countries *The Unfortunate Traveller* suggests travelers should avoid is entirely European: direct exposure to the East does not even appear as a possibility.

Nashe's Jews are stereotypically drawn: Jack explains the motives of Zadoch by saying that "all Iewes are couetous" (304). This motive differs from the economic motivation for "the Turke" in the *Farewell* in that Riche's narrator will supply an explanation for "the Turke's" need for money; we see no such need in Zadoch. He acts from greed, which Nashe feels no need to explain and which reflects a relatively uncomplicated view of the colonized culture.

Nashe's work—while it retains conventional stereotypes of the East—becomes complicated in an intriguing fashion. Arthur F. Kinney has noted in a different context that the only physical description we receive of Jack Wilton is given by Zadoch.[14] We learn that Jack is "of the age of eighteene, of stature tall, straight limd, of as cleare a complection as any Painters fancie can imagine" (2:304). Zadoch provides this description because he is trying—quite literally—to objectify Jack. He wants to sell the Englishman to Doctor Zacharie as the subject for the doctor's yearly demonstration of anatomy. The use of the Eastern culture as Other thus becomes extremely problematic: we know Jack's appearance (what he physically "is") only because of his appearance to the Other. Jack himself is apparently in no position to know his external nature. Simultaneously, Zadoch describes Jack's external self while attempting to persuade Zacharie to buy Jack in order to dissect him in order to examine and describe his inner self. The East becomes an essential element in the process of self-definition. And Jack's response to this threatened examination is prayer and fear. It would seem that *The Unfortunate Traveller* presents an English response to colonizing impulses turned against them. *The Unfortunate Traveller*, under the guise of objective scientific scrutiny (a phrase that is, of course, qualified because it refers to the actions of the stereotyped Jews), turns the colonizer (Jack, who provides the colonizing narrative voice) into the colonized. Kinney has suggested that the Roman episode functions as "Jack's last and decisive lesson before his return to the English,"[15] and one reason that this is true is that in Rome the colonization process has been faced and reversed.

II

Whereas Painter, Munday, and Nashe provide their readers with stereotypical responses to the East, Riche's treatment in the *Farewell* provides a more complex system of responses that problematize the writer's relation to his text and his readers' relation to their society. The most obvious—and most difficult—place to begin an examination of Riche's colonization of the Ottoman Empire is with "Aramanthus borne a Leper," since "the greate Turke" (168) and his armies are prominent characters in it. The argument of the story, the seventh in the *Farewell*, is as follows:

> *Aramanthus* soonne to *Rodericke* Kyng of *Tolosia,* beeyng borne a Leper, was sent by his father to the Isle of *Candy* for remedie, and by a tempeste at the Sea, the Shippe was driuen into *Turkie,* where she was cast awaie, and no manne saued but the childe, whiche was taken vp by a poore Fisherman, and fostered as his owne soonne, and afterwardes seruyng the Turke in his warres, shewed hym self so politique that the Turke by his onely aduise, incroched muche vpon the Christians, and in fine by his meane the Citie of *Tolosia* was taken, his father put in prison, and how in the ende he was knowne to bee the soonne of *Rodericke.* (166)

This argument provides a fairly accurate summary of the narrative, except that it ignores the role of Queen Isabell, who has already been discussed in relation to Riche's anxieties about female power. The difficulties inherent in the portrayal of the Turks here are evident as soon as they enter the story. The first Turk we meet is the fisherman who saves Aramanthus, becomes his foster father, and restores his health: "He [the fisherman] tooke it [the baby Aramanthus] vp in his armes, and cariyng it home, with Bathes and homely Oyntmentes of his owne deuising, within a very little space, the childe was restored to perfecte health" (167). This Turk evades "Reprobate" status (to use Newton's term). He is instead a stock figure familiar to us from *Oedipus, Daphnis and Chloe,* and *The Winter's Tale.* The narrative suggests, however, that we should not accord to this fisherman the unqualified praise that is usually attributed to these characters. When the adult Aramanthus desires to become a soldier in the Turk's army, the narrator tells us that "his father the Fisherman was greatly displeased, and beganne to preache vnto his sonne of the incommodities of warre, and with how many miseries Souldiers are besieged" (168). The fisherman's sentiments are given a negative value in the *Farewell*.

The narrative voice of the prefatory material and "Sappho Duke of Mantona" have criticized either implicitly or explicitly English society's disrespect for the military life. As the prefatory material makes plain, the *Farewell* is written because the narrator believes that soldiers are no longer respected in the decadent Elizabethan period and feels that he must accede to cultural fashion and "followe the course of the worlde" (10). Placing criticism of a desire for the military life into the mouth of the fisherman recalls those characters in "Sappho" who similarly devalued the worth of a soldier, and it should prompt suspicions of the Turkish fisherman's argument.

As readers, however, we cannot discredit the character of the fisherman completely. The nurturing characteristics he has exhibited cannot be completely negated by the "tradition" of distrust for the nonmilitary in which Riche's *Farewell* participates. We find ourselves supporting the nonmilitaristic tradition the fisherman represents even in the face of narrative disapproval. Identification with the Turkish fisherman at this point in the story is made psychologically problematic by the stereotyping of Ottomans as heathen "Reprobates" who were identified bodily with the anti-Christ (while, according to Luther, the Pope was "the spirit or soul of the anti-Christ"[16]). The readers' difficulties assimilating the positive qualities of the Turks become even more troublesome as the narrative continues.

Assimilation of the reader to Eastern culture—or projection onto it of all that belongs to a society of "Reprobates"—becomes difficult because "the greate Turke" and the Turkish fisherman do not remain static figures. Early in the text, the Turkish ruler (who is never named but who can probably be identified with Suleiman the Magnificent) is "evil" from the European/Christian point of view because he wars with the surrounding peoples, but these hostile actions are mitigated by two factors. First, the victories of his armies are the result of Aramanthus's "counsaill" and "aduise" (168): it is really the nobility of the orphaned European which allows "the Turke" to perform "wonderfull spoiles vpon the Christians" (168). Secondly, Riche presents a motive for his behavior, and it is not the racist attribution of a natural hatred toward Christians to which Fenton refers[17] or to the underhanded actions inherent in "Reprobate" peoples. Instead, his motive is purely economic, and it is a motive Riche's readers could have understood: "the Turke" has a daughter whose "name was *Florella*, whose beautie was verie excellent, and minding to matche his daughter with some noble Prince, he pretented that suche Countries, Cities, Tounes, Castelles, Fortes, or what so euer he could by conquest get from the Christians, to giue them all for his daughters dowrie" (168). Admittedly, the dowry resulting from this plan would be huge—perhaps larger than we are expected to believe necessary (and it is possible, too, to construct a more sinister reading of this passage by working with the meanings of "pretented"). But the relevant point here is that "the Turke," for all his cultural differences and the threat he poses to the Tolosians, is endowed in this instance with the same desires for his daughter as the Europeans have for theirs. (Remember, too, that one of the most vivid scenes in Riche's *Farewell* is the scene in "Nicander and Lucilla" in which Lucilla's mother argues herself into selling her daughter's virginity in order to provide her with a dowry.) This motivated view of "the greate Turke's" actions enters the nexus of views already present in Riche's culture where it does not overthrow the perception of the evil Easterner, but helps prepare the reader not to accept his or her assumptions about the Ottoman rulers.

"The greate Turke" does, of course, eventually prove his evil and godless nature: he fakes a conversion to Christianity and demonstrates his blasphemy by receiving a baptism in which he does not believe and by requesting that all his men undergo the same ritual. The phony conversion is followed by his feigned death, which permits his soldiers to stage a funeral in Tolosia, which custom demands they attend carrying their weapons. Once inside the city walls, the Ottoman soldiers attack, "the Turke" rises from his coffin, and Tolosia is captured after a bloody battle. This view of the Ottoman Empire—that it is sacrilegious and barbarous and will use any strategem, no matter how nefarious, to conquer Christians—must contend with the goodness of the fisherman who raises Aramanthus and with the final acts of "the Turke." In the last scene in the narrative, he restores Tolosia to

King Rodericke, frees Queen Isabell, and allows Aramanthus to marry his daughter, regardless of his resulting financial loss. More significantly, and some might say amazingly, "the Turke . . . became in deede to be Christened, with all his retinew that was aboute hym," and then "departed with his armie into Turkie" (179).[18] Any attempt to read this text as a historical chronicle ends here. The entrance of the Turks into the Christian world (and so, one surmises, the abolition of Islam), did not happen. Yet this concluding gesture creates a certain sense of closure: it imposes a sense of circularity, of return to stasis from the very threatening events the "greate Turke" causes.

How then can we read the ending of "Aramanthus"? It is first necessary to focus on the initial threat the Turks pose to the Tolosians. King Rodericke is initially wary of them, but his hesitancy drops after the baptism and the "death" of "the Turke." This loosening of relations between the two peoples demonstrates a blurring of the us/them, same/other boundaries that are seen most clearly along religious lines and which then become obliterated by the boundary-crossing process of baptism. Religion and culture are near equivalents in this example, so the process by which they accept our faith makes them no different from us. This argument makes no accommodation for cultural differences or the need for political expediency: because we (the Tolosians) see this baptism as a sacred act not to be undertaken lightly, the Ottomans must feel similarly.

What does this interpretation suggest in relation to Riche's readers' perception of the alien in "Aramanthus" and the tendency to project fears and anxieties onto the Other? First, it seems to suggest insecurity about their own economic power (remember that the motivation given for "the greate Turke's" invasions is to raise a dowry). Economic sympathy with a version of the Turkish ruler's position seems to spark a wholesale identification with him, spurred on by our experience with the kindly Turkish fisherman who raises Aramanthus. This identification is confirmed by the ritual of the first baptism. The faked "rebirth" of "the Turke" and the bloodshed that accompanies it signal difficulties with the colonizing process. The easy equation of the goals of other countries with our own is shown to be in reality a distorting and diminishing of the colonized group's intentions. The violent takeover of Tolosia chastises the reader for equating Turkish and Tolosian goals as Rodericke and his counselors did. The extremes to which the Tolosians are driven in order to survive their conquest by the Turks (for example, the breast-feeding of Rodericke by Isabell) are evidence of the error of assuming that "they" are like "us." The final, fictional conversion of the Turks to Christianity *should* be met with resistance by the reader: we know it defies our knowledge of history and we know what happened the last time we believed in such a baptism. The conclusion of the narrative, in other words, can be read as an attempt to accept the proposition that "we" and "they" can be united, but only on "our" terms (Christianity) and only in a form which our historical knowledge prevents us from believing: it is a union only possible in fiction.

"Aramanthus" need not be read only as indicating the impossibility of eradicating the differences between Eastern and Western cultures. It also questions the methods and semiotic indicators used to separate our definitions of Eastern cultures and Western cultures, of "us" and "them." Given what we know of Barnabe Riche's background—his precarious financial background, his time spent in Ireland, his eagerness to seek preferment at court—and given the popular, non-aristocratic nature of the *Farewell,* it is hard to imagine Riche identifying "us"—the desired, privileged group—with the Tolosians. They are, after all, a beseiged people plagued by internal conflict (the jealousy and envy that destroy harmony at court). Nor does Tolosian society provide a fertile ground in which Aramanthus can achieve his aristocratic potential, for his prowess is only developed by his interaction with the Turks. The Turks, conversely, have only minor problems. They may be economically in need, but then so was the English aristocracy in Riche's England. The Turks are militarily strong and internally harmonious, even down to the level of the poor fisherman; they seem to have all—except Christianity—that the Tolosians desire. The final baptism of the Turks, then, may signal a recognition that Riche's readers may eventually join the powerful, ruling class. That union will not, however, come without a very high cost: the blaspheming of Christianity and the identification with the anti-Christ Other implied by the baptism of the Turks.

This interpretation is not fully satisfying. Because Riche has the Turks abandon a significant aspect of their culture, there is a suggestion here that accommodation must come not from the class of Riche's readers (who desire to gain the status and power of the aristocracy or, analogously, the Turks), but rather from that aristocracy itself. It is not Riche's readers who "lose" part of their identity; that loss is reserved for the ruling class. The implications of this scheme are subversive, at least subconsciously. What is implied by "Aramanthus" is a change in the power structure of Riche's England to adjust to the new power of the Tolosians—the merchant- and craftsman-based classes Stevenson discusses in *Praise and Paradox*. This analysis echoes critics such as Karl, Margolies, and (in a sense) Walter R. Davis, who have seen fiction in general or Elizabethan novelistic discourse specifically as subversive of power relations in early modern England. Riche's treatment of these issues in "Aramanthus" seems to suggest serious anxieties about that subversive process. To have the aristocratic class accommodate itself to the new power of the merchant class is, perhaps, mildly subversive, but to turn that aristocratic class whose power is desired into the Turks, the embodiment of the anti-Christ, seems to indicate extreme dissatisfaction with the options and opportunities available to Riche's readers. To have the Turks abandon Islam and adopt Christianity is to move in the direction of accepting the options for power available to Riche's readers, but it does not dispel the problems inherent in colonizing that culture for use as a symbol of middle-class desires. The Otherness of the Turks in "Aramanthus" simultaneously attracts and repels Riche's readers even as it both nurtures and oppresses the narrative's European characters.

In a somewhat different manner, the Tunisians and Moors of "Fineo and Fiamma" likewise appeal to and repulse the reader. We have noticed that Riche's use of description and setting in "Fineo and Fiamma" allows him to define different kinds of societies, and Eastern cultures are strongly implicated in this process. Unlike its treatment in "Aramanthus," however, the East is less ambivalently presented in "Fineo and Fiamma." The only attractions the East holds in this text are those of piratical law—especially its sense that one's strength will always be rewarded if it proves victorious—and of the comfort of a law based on tradition. Attraction is not, however, identification: "Fineo and Fiamma" provides its readers with little reason to identify with the East. Although there may be a desire among the readership to return to a tradition-based legal system, and although wealth accompanies Eastern culture, the blasphemy of the King of Tunis's "Cube" tends to subvert any desire the reader may have to be accepted into and identify with that culture. Both of Riche's narratives present a longing for a connection—or re-connection—with the East, but that longing is mitigated in "Fineo and Fiamma" to a much greater extent than it is in "Aramanthus." "Fineo and Fiamma" also lessens considerably the threat posed by the East since its European social order and characters remain largely unchanged (except that the two lovers have achieved in the East the wedding Western culture prevented). The wedding of the two characters causes no wider implications for societal definitions or definitions of corporate identity. In "Aramanthus," on the other hand, the primary European characters gain their identity because of the Turks' presence, and the final baptism of "the Turke" and his soldiers ensures that society will always display the effects of this union.

"Sappho Duke of Mantona" and "Apolonius and Silla" also demonstrate the role of the East in the creation of their characters' identities, but they do so in a much less complicated manner. In each text, the primary male character has, before the narrative begins, established his reputation by fighting the Turks. Both become known as valiant soldiers through their experience with the East—and they are known as soldiers who are accustomed to a "soft" courtier's life (that is why, for instance, Apolonius engages Cesario/Silla to woo Julina in "Apolonius and Silla"). In both these works, the East presents a place in which male characters establish their individual identity as military heroes but lose their connection to their societies' collective sense of self: the postwar societies to which they return no longer valorize the military heroes they urged them to become.

The threat of the East is reported, not dramatized, in these narratives, but its effects are nonetheless horrendous: in both tales characters lose their names and their socioeconomic status, and they must struggle to retain even slight links to their cultures. Sappho, for instance, loses his wife, son, and daughter and must work under an assumed name as a church beadle in a foreign country until such time as a renewed threat by "the Turke" causes a revalution of military power. Silla, in her tale, loses her money, rank, family, and gender because of the self "the Turke" has created for Apolonius. Notice that it is not Apolonius whose culture is destroyed by his involvement with the East; it is Silla who loses identity. Nevertheless, Apolonius's need to hire a boy who can act the role of courtly lover, a role he cannot fill, suggests the ability of "the Turke" to destroy the individual's sense of societal identity. Although this second text presents a converse of the paradigm "Sappho" provides, the general principles of involvement with the East in these two texts seem clear: defining oneself in relation to the East yields loss of collective identity and isolation from one's class. "The Turke" need not even appear in the narrative for society's nature to be radically altered by his existence. The desire to identify with the East on even this minimal level (that is, to become a soldier and compete in the area of the Ottoman Empire's expertise) causes destruction of class identity and isolation from one's class. It simultaneously provokes and denies self-definition or class identification.

III

Eastern cultures present writers and readers of Elizabethan novelistic discourse with an Other that must be subdued and controlled if they are to establish their own notions of identity. The simplest response, like that of Munday's *Zelauto* and Painter's novellas, allows the reader to objectify the East without qualification. The East then becomes an abstract field in which idealized aspects of identity (Christianity, nobility, duty, etc.) can flourish in a context that acts to reassure the reader and writer of the strength and validity of conventional values. Riche's view of the East problematizes this approach to the boundaries between East and West. Riche describes an East that allows the European to develop his or her strengths, but it is an East that also destroys the cultural bases of much of what provides the foundation of collective Western identity. It is not Nashe's East, which presents no benefit for the European. We must recoil, with Jack Wilton, from Nashe's East; we must come to terms with Riche's.

Conclusion

Novelistic Discourse & the Problem of Realism

—

> If the basic convention governing the novel is the expectation that readers will, through their contact with the text, be able to recognize a world which it produces or to which it refers, it ought to be possible to identify at least some elements of the text whose function it is to confirm this expectation and to assert the representational or mimetic orientation of fiction.
>
> —Jonathan Culler, "Poetics of the Novel"

IT IS TO CONCERNS such as Culler raises that any study of Elizabethan novelistic discourse must ultimately come. Culler's essay both begins and ends with an emphasis on the novel's "basic convention": the novel "produces" or "refers to" a world that readers will be able to recognize. The process of recognition is qualified by tensions within the novel that produce moments of "recognition and dislocation" that create the reader's interest in the fiction: we understand the novel's world, but we cannot quite predict events and character behavior within it.[1] That process of recognition and dislocation identifies the central function of novelistic discourse within the world of its readers and writers.

This study is in part designed to indicate ways in which Elizabethan novelistic discourse adheres to Culler's "basic convention." The focus is not primarily on the "representational or mimetic orientation" of these texts; instead, it identifies diverse strategies by which those who produced and were produced by the prose fictions of the Elizabethan period in England were authorized to engage in simultaneous recognition with and dislocation from their culture. Especially central to this inquiry is the role of non-aristocratic readers, readers who were able to see within these texts a critique of an English society that still clung to the vestiges of feudal traditions. Fictions by such writers as Barnabe Riche, George Gascoigne, Thomas Deloney, Sir Philip Sidney, John Lyly, Thomas Lodge, Robert Greene, and Thomas Nashe demonstrate the concerns of readers trying to accustom themselves to their increasingly modern world at the same time that they illustrate the artistically and socially precarious position of their writers. In writing for the marketplace, as most of these writers did, they marked themselves as below the gentry at the same time that a primary goal of their writings, as their prefaces often show, was to gain preferment or court patronage.

This two-fold attempt to authorize both the position of the writers and the readers of Elizabethan novelistic discourse establishes its adherence to Culler's "basic convention." Although romances such as Lodge's *Rosalynde* or Sidney's *Arcadia* may not establish a mimetic correspondence with persons or places within late Elizabethan England, they nonetheless represent problems and concerns typical to the period. Readers could explore through these texts political anxieties caused by changes in class structures and domestic economic dependencies, external threats (such as that posed by the Spanish Armada in 1588), and, as the childless queen aged, increasing worry over the succession of the crown. Through reading about the restoration of Lodge's Rosalynd and her father to power, readers could rehearse various approaches to questions of political control and the role of women within English culture and the ruling elite, and they could acknowledge the lingering doubts the text's conclusion presents. The kind of world that romances such as *Arcadia* or *Rosalynde* produce is perhaps not as mimetic as that of Greene's cony-catching pamphlets, but that difference in "realism" is not significant. Both texts allow writers and readers to "recognize a world" within those texts; both texts permit writers and readers to create positions for themselves in the worlds the texts describe. Both authorize the writers' and the readers' attempts at defining themselves and their position within English culture.

One final point needs to be addressed in relation to the connection between Elizabethan novelistic discourse and definitions of the novel. Culler finds in the novel moments when we are unable to predict the action of the plot, regardless of how fully we are able to recognize the world the novelist has created. These moments of "dislocation" are key to the reading process: they keep us interested and keep us convinced that the author knows more about the characters and text than we do. The traditional plots and lack of individualized characters in Elizabethan novelistic discourse are often seen as preventing such "dislocation." Predictability, in this assessment of the operation of fiction, is a negative quality. But Elizabethan novelistic discourse, one could argue, is no more predictable than novels in any other period in English literary history. The murder of Thomas Cole in *Thomas of Reading* is unexpected, as is Jack Wilton's involvement with the Jewish anatomists in Rome. Nonetheless, although the reading of novels may in part be motivated by a desire to find out what happens next, it is also motivated by a desire to obtain confirmation of our sense of how the plot *should* develop. That readers have such desires is obvious from the popularity of detective stories, popular romances, and science fiction. Readers of these texts derive considerable pleasure by anticipating ways in which events that they know must happen *do* happen, from observing ways in which authors they have read before work into the novels characteristic phrases or pieces of information, and from seeing to what degree they can correctly anticipate the events of the text.[2]

Elizabethan novelistic discourse may adhere more closely to this model of reading. Observing the ways in which the author handles the separation of the royal child from its parents, the banishment of the rightful ruler from his kingdom, or the eventual restoration of the lost child to its aristocratic parents furnishes readers with pleasures similar to those we derive from contemporary generic fiction. The ways in which authors negotiate these aspects of their plots provide the necessary interest for reading to continue: the authors' specific variations within the larger framework of the genre create different means by which writers and readers may experiment with a variety of solutions to somewhat formulaic situations. This tendency exists in sixteenth-century fiction and in later fiction as well. We know, for instance, that Elizabeth Bennett and Darcy will eventually marry, that Catherine and Heathcliff will be separated, that Oliver Twist will be revealed to be the child of highborn parents, and that Jake Barnes and Lady Brett Ashley will be no happier at the end of *The Sun Also Rises* than they are at its beginning. This predictability, this genre-knowledge, creates much of the pleasure provided by the fictional text. Novelistic discourse, whether early modern or postmodern, provokes its effects through the tension between the formulaic and the unknown, the typical and the individual, the self and the Other.

Notes

INTRODUCTION
Elizabethan Contexts and Generic Anxiety

1. Paul Salzman, *English Prose Fiction 1558-1700: A Critical History*, 5-6. Salzman provides a thorough analysis of the various fictional prose genres popular during the period.

2. See, however, Jeffrey Kittay and Wlad Godzich's *The Emergence of Prose: An Essay in Prosaics*, a work to which I am greatly indebted. Kittay and Godzich argue that the shift from poetry to prose as the default mode of discourse occurs as part of the shift to a textual culture required by changes in the organization of the state. As the reading of texts becomes more important culturally, prose gains dominance.

3. See William Baldwin, Beware the Cat: *The First English Novel*.

4. Alastair Fowler, "The Life and Death of Literary Forms," 86-87; Lennard J. Davis, *Factual Fictions: The Origins of the English Novel;* Michael McKeon, *The Origins of the English Novel, 1600-1740*, 26-27; Earl Miner, "Some Issues of Literary 'Species or Distinct Kind'"; Margaret Spufford, *Small Books and Pleasant Histories: Popular Fiction and Its Readership in Seventeenth-Century England*, 262-67. Miner also cautions against establishing rash and imprecise generic categories. Yet he acknowledges a culture's need to formulate distinct categories while simultaneously recognizing that our terminology is by nature imprecise, that categories overlap, and that concensus is hard to reach: "It appears to me that we shall never agree that 'genre' means thus-and-so. The meaning, not the name, is the important thing" (25).

5. M. M. Bakhtin, *The Dialogic Imagination*, 369, 370; Georg Lukács, *The Theory of the Novel*, chap. 3.

6. References to Riche's text will be by page number to *Rich's Farewell to Military Profession (1581)*, edited by T. M. Cranfill.

7. David Margolies, *Novel and Society in Elizabethan England*, vii.

8. T. M. Cranfill and Dorothy Bruce, *Barnaby Rich: A Short Biography;* John Leon Lievsay, "A Word about Barnaby Rich," 384-85; Roland Barthes, "Introduction to the Structural Analysis of Narratives," 287.

9. Lievsay, 388, 387; Margaret Schlauch, *Antecedents of the English Novel, 1400-1600: From Chaucer to Deloney,* 149, 151, 160. Suzanne Hull, *Chaste, Silent and Obedient: English Books for Women, 1475-1600,* 197. For studies of Riche's narratives as dramatic sources, see Warner G. Rice, "The Moroccan Episode in Thomas Heywood's *The Fair Maid of the West,"* and James Craigie, *"Philotus:* A Late Middle Scots Comedy." The most recent scholarly work on Riche's *Farewell,* Donald Beecher's substantial introduction to the 1992 edition, came into my hands too late to be thoroughly incorporated into this study.

10. Walter R. Davis, *Idea and Act in Elizabethan Fiction,* 159. See also the assessments of Riche's *Farewell* in studies ranging from J. J. Jusserand's *The English Novel in the Time of Shakespeare* (1890) to the more recent analyses of Margolies, Salzman, and Arthur F. Kinney, *Humanist Poetics: Thought, Rhetoric, and Fiction in Sixteenth-Century England.*

11. Jacqueline T. Miller, *Poetic License: Authority and Authorship in Medieval and Renaissance Contexts.*

12. Sir Philip Sidney, *A Defence of Poetry,* 19; subsequent references are to this edition. Francis Bacon, *The Advancement of Learning,* Book 2, in Joel E. Spingarn, ed., *Critical Essays of the Seventeenth Century,* 5; George Puttenham, *The Arte of English Poesie,* 56. In "Defining Non-Fiction Genres," Ann Imbrie discusses the devaluation of sixteenth- and seventeenth-century English nonfiction, citing Sidney and Puttenham as evidence that prose during the period was valued more than is conventionally thought. Imbrie's primary concern is, as her title suggests, with nonfiction; consequently, her analysis does not extend to the texts under consideration here. Anne Drury Hall, in *Ceremony and Civility in English Renaissance Prose,* similarly argues that sixteenth-century English prose deserves greater critical attention. Her work also limits itself primarily to examples of nonfiction.

13. George Gascoigne, "Certayne Notes of Instruction" 1:52; Gabriel Harvey, *Foure Letters* 2:229-38; Thomas Nashe, "Preface to Greene's *Menaphon,"* in *The Works of Thomas Nashe* 3:300-10. Harvey, in criticizing Robert Greene's work, wishes the reading public "had either more Reason to discerne, or lesse Appetite to desire such Nouels" (2:231).

14. Attitudes toward courtly and theatrical audiences were clear. In his introduction to *Menaphon by Robert Greene* and *A Margarite of America by Thomas Lodge,* editor G. B. Harrison reminds his readers of the contempt Greene felt for Marlowe when Marlowe left the ranks of the university wits and chose to write for the theater (vi). While Greene may have been critical of Marlowe's mercenary shift in artistic focus, he later wrote for the theater himself.

15. Laura Caroline Stevenson, *Praise and Paradox: Merchants and Craftsmen in Elizabethan Popular Literature,* esp. 51-74; Louis B. Wright, *Middle-Class Culture in Elizabethan England;* Lawrence Stone, *The Crisis of the Aristocracy,* 389. Although Wright's work has been criticized for its overly inclusive and anachronistic definition of the Elizabethan middle class that romanticizes the period (implicit in Margolies, *Novel and Society,* 17) and for overestimating the degree of feminism in the late sixteenth century (Mary Ellen Lamb, *Gender and Authorship in the Sidney Circle,* 226 n. 37), his work remains an important catalog of Elizabethan readers' and

writers' interests. Stone has also received considerable criticism in the recent past for his reliance on anecdotes and a smaller body of factual data than many would like. Nonetheless, his contribution to our understanding of social structures during the period is undeniably considerable. Although this study refers to Elizabethan novelistic discourse and its readers, I do not intend to deny that these texts were frequently read aloud to an audience. In most cases the reception of the texts in the instances I describe would be roughly similar for both groups. See Walter J. Ong's *Orality and Literacy: Technologizing the Word* for a discussion of the fundamental issues involved. William Nelson's "'From Listen Lordings' to 'Dear Reader'" and Margolies's *Novel and Society* consider these texts as primarily oral in the first case and in transition from oral to literate in the second.

16. See, for instance, Keith Wrightson, *English Society 1580-1680*; Elizabeth L. Eisenstein, *The Printing Press as an Agent of Change;* Christopher Hill, *Reformation to Industrial Revolution;* and Spufford, *Small Books and Pleasant Histories.*

17. Margolies, *Novel and Society,* 10, 11.

18. Spufford, *Small Books,* 22, 32, 34, 51, 55-60; David Cressy, "Educational Opportunity in Tudor and Stuart England," 314. Cressy's figures are for East Anglia rather than England as a whole. During the same period, he finds that 56 percent of craftsmen and tradesmen were literate and that "merchants and superior shopkeepers... could have an illiteracy level as low as 6-12%" (314). Hill describes the period's growing emphasis on education as an outgrowth of the Protestant belief in the importance of vernacular reading. He describes how in spite of the endowment of grammar schools and the growing number of non-aristocrats in universities during the mid-sixteenth century, the gentry gradually pushed lower-class children out of the village schools and, consequently, the university (*Reformation to Revolution,* 38-40, 206-7).

In discussing the eighteenth-century reading public, Ian Watt identifies servants and apprentices as two groups having a greater chance of reading fiction than some other members of the working class because they had access to books without necessarily having to buy them, a greater disposable income than some other groups (should they have wanted to purchase books), and more leisure time while on the job (*The Rise of the Novel,* 47). Perhaps, on a somewhat smaller scale, this conclusion may be extended backwards into the Elizabethan period.

19. See Spufford, *Small Books*; Louis B. Wright, *Middle-Class Culture.* Girls were not taught the same subjects as their male counterparts, nor did they remain in school for the same length of time. Nonetheless, reading was taught to some non-aristocratic girls (Spufford, 34), an important fact in light of Margaret L. King's conclusion that there were only sixty humanistically educated women in Tudor England (*Women of the Renaissance,* 208).

20. Suzanne Hull's research uncovered twenty-four books aimed at a female audience published before 1573, nineteen published between 1573 and 1582, eighteen published between 1583 and 1592, and twenty-four published between 1593 and 1602 (*Chaste,* 7). Stevenson reads Hull's study cautiously, suggesting that female literacy may have been generally restricted to the upper classes (*Praise and Paradox,* 64-65). See also Louis B. Wright, "The Reading of Renaissance English Women," 140-41.

On the other hand, Joan Kelly-Gadol's influential "Did Women Have a Renaissance?" discusses in part the effect the growth of humanism had on the education of women in Renaissance Italy. She sees educational opportunities for women decreasing during the period because women lost direct access both to education and to the example the educated great lady presented in medieval courts. Under humanist influence, education for women began to consist of training by their brothers' tutors in a system of thought that "suppressed romance and chivalry to further classical culture, with all its patriarchal and misogynous bias" (152). Lisa Jardine also discusses the effect of humanist education on women and stresses its availability only to upper-class women and the emphasis it placed on subjects that could be called decorative rather than useful (*Still Harping on Daughters: Women and Drama in the Age of Shakespeare,* 51–56). See also Dale Spender, *Mothers of the Novel: 100 Good Women Writers before Jane Austen,* 16.

21. Louis B. Wright cites the second example as evidence that lower-class women may not routinely have been taught to read ("The Reading of Renaissance English Women," 142–43).

22. Frank Whigham, *Ambition and Privilege: The Social Tropes of Elizabethan Courtesy Theory,* 31; Stephen Greenblatt, *Renaissance Self-Fashioning: From More to Shakespeare,* 9.

CHAPTER 1
Prose, Poetry, and Popular Authority

1. William Nelson, *Fact or Fiction: The Dilemma of the Renaissance Storyteller,* 98.

2. Jacopo Sannazaro, *Arcadia and Piscatorial Eclogues,* 10. The date its most recent editor gives for the publication of a "good" edition of the text, although the work was written at least fifteen years earlier, is 1504.

3. The model for my conclusions here is Stanley E. Fish's sense of the reading process and the constantly changing interpretations it produces, especially as described in "Interpreting the Variorum" (147–73). References to Lodge's text are by page number to Harrison's edition.

4. Salzman, in *Prose Fiction* (78), and Ernest A. Baker, in *The History of the English Novel* (119), call *Margarite* a romance. Lodge's text calls itself a "history" (113). Walter R. Davis finds it indebted to the Greek romance for its *in medias res* opening but argues that "it soon settles down to the more familiar Euphuistic model" (*Idea and Act,* 199). Kinney terms it a "humanist fiction of felicity" (*Humanist Poetics,* 300). See also the introduction to James Clyde Addison, Jr.'s *An Old-Spelling Critical Edition of Thomas Lodge's* A Margarite of America *(1596),* which places it solidly within the romance tradition and which discusses the specific Italian poets and poems to which Lodge refers (243–47). Esther Garke's *The Use of Songs in Elizabethan Fiction* provides a structural assessment of songs and poems within texts such as Lodge's *Margarite* and the contexts in which these poems are found. Richard Helgerson interprets the *Margarite* poems quite differently from Garke or myself, seeing in them evidence of Lodge's growing disenchantment with poetry. He asserts that the poetry must be seen as representative of Lodge's character as much as of the character to whom they are ascribed (117). On mannerism, see James V. Mirollo's *Mannerism and Renaissance Poetry: Concept, Mode, Inner Design* and John M. Steadman's *Redefining a Period Style: "Renaissance," "Mannerist" and "Baroque" in Literature.*

Lodge's *Margarite* bears on the argument of this study in many significant ways. Its emphasis on "fashioning" ties it to Barnabe Riche's concerns with self-presentation; its dedication to "Ladie Russell" places it among the small group of early modern texts intended for a primarily female audience; and, most strikingly, its setting in "America" aligns it with those Elizabethan prose fictions concerned with foreign cultures.

5. References to Deloney's texts are by page number to Merritt Lawlis's edition of *The Novels of Thomas Deloney*. For a recent discussion of some of *Jack*'s poetry, especially its ballads, see Joan Pong Linton, "*Jack of Newbery* [sic] and Drake in California: Domestic and Colonial Narratives of English Cloth and Manhood." Lyly's *Euphues* provides a similar example of a prose narrative that authorizes itself by the use of traditional literary forms. Structured more like a series of classical orations than a dialogic discourse, Lyly avoids the need for poetry's authority altogether. He does, however, conclude his work with a series of prose epistles that act to connect the text to the "literature of education" (Janel Mueller, *The Native Tongue and the Word: Developments in English Prose Style, 1380–1580*, 387).

6. Virginia Woolf, "*The Countess of Pembroke's Arcadia*," 37–38.

7. In *George Gascoigne: Elizabethan Courtier, Soldier, and Poet*, C. T. Prouty concludes that the poems were written before the prose portions of the text and that they were based on an affair Gascoigne had in the mid-1550s (196–98); *George Gascoigne's A Hundreth Sundrie Flowres*, 243. My argument does not depend on the autobiographical nature of the text, but the connection between Gascoigne's life and work may be seen to amplify my case. The implication of this link is that poetry is itself insufficient to explain and create narratives of experience. Poetry provides the grounding for narratives, but prose is needed to make them complete. For further discussion of poetry's reliance on prose to complete narratives in the modern world, see Kittay and Godzich, *Emergence of Prose*, especially chapter 7. G. T.'s references to Dame Pergo, like the prose linking the text's poems, calls into question Woolf's view of poems as the realistic core of such narratives. G. T. presents "Pergo" as a pseudonym for a "gentlewoman of the company whom I have not hitherto named, and that for good respects, least hir name might altogether disclose" the identity of the characters who hide behind initials (George Gascoigne, *A Discourse of the Adventures Passed by Master F. J.*, 87).

8. On the text as a study of interpretive strategies, see, for example, George E. Rowe, Jr.'s "Interpretation, Sixteenth-Century Readers and George Gascoigne's 'The Adventures of Master F.J.'" and M. R. Rohr Philmus's "Gascoigne's Fable of the Artist as a Young Man."

9. Bakhtin, *Dialogic Imagination*, 67. Margaret Schlauch, in "English Short Fiction in the 15th and 16th Centuries," includes the *Mirror* in a discussion of the morally didactic aims of early fiction. Heather Dubrow's "A Mirror for Complaints" explores the relation between the *Mirror* and the complaint genre as a whole. I am also indebted to an unpublished essay by Thomas M. O'Shea that discusses the *Mirror* along somewhat similar lines.

10. Kittay and Godzich, *Emergence of Prose*, 158. For a useful analysis of *The Rape of Lucrece* and the importance of its prose argument, see Nancy Vickers, "'The blazon of sweet beauty's best': Shakespeare's *Lucrece*," 95–115.

11. Miner, "Some Issues," 37. Barbara Herrnstein Smith, in "Poetry as Fiction," would seem to agree. She splits modes of discourse into "natural utterances," which she defines as "the verbal responses of an historically real person, occasioned and determined by an historically real universe" (170-71), and "fictive utterances" in which "the speaking, addressing, expressing and alluding [performed by their speaker] are themselves fictive verbal acts" (177). Renaissance theorists, as we have seen, are also willing to hedge on this question.

12. It should be noted that a third tale, "Twoo Brethren and Their Wiues," also contains an embedded text, but, like the final embedded document in Deloney's *Jack of Newbury*, it is a prose letter. Its appearance, in the fifth segment of the *Farewell*, may suggest that after the earlier uses of poetry in the work, poetry has run its course. The gradual shift away from poetry as the *Farewell* progresses may also reflect Riche's changing relation to the romance genre. In *The Straunge and Wonderfull Aduentures of Don Simonides* Riche constructs a lengthy romance that includes several embedded poems. In 1592, however, Riche published another romance, *The Aduentures of Brusanus Prince of Hungaria*, from which poetry is entirely absent.

13. Esther Garke briefly discusses the poetry in "Sappho," but she does so in the context of a description of the "singers" of songs within courtly settings. She finds that Riche devotes an unusually long portion of the text to the process of composing, memorizing, and performing a love song (*Use of Songs*, 22).

14. Kinney, *Humanist Poetics*, 213; Riche, *Farewell*, xvii-xxi. For more detailed discussion of "Sappho"'s sources, see D. T. Starnes, "Barnabe Riche's 'Sappho Duke of Mantona': A Study in Elizabethan Story-Making," as well as T. M. Cranfill's "Barnaby Rich's 'Sappho' and *The Weakest Goeth to the Wall.*"

15. Another significant question this text raises is that of the effect of source material on Elizabethan novelistic discourse. This tale is based on a novella by Giraldi Cinthio, and Cranfill identifies Don Hercules as based on one of Cinthio's patrons, Ercole II, son of Lucrezia Borgia (Riche, *Farewell*, 276); the positive reading Riche gives Don Hercules's actions may stem from this fact.

16. Riche, *Farewell*, 255.

17. Ibid., 278.

18. Such a conclusion is only possible when the text's narrative voice manipulates its readers into accepting this Macchiavellian premise based on an objectification of the female.

19. See, especially, Stone's observation that "money was the means of acquiring and retaining status, but it was not the essence of it: the acid test was the mode of life" (*Crisis of the Aristocracy*, 50).

20. On Riche's relation to his female readers, see Caroline Lucas, *Writing for Women: The Example of Woman as Reader of Elizabethan Romance*, 95-117. In discussing "Nicander and Lucilla," Lucas emphasizes Riche's focus on the power of chastity.

21. The empowerment of readers was more important for Lodge and Riche than Sidney, whose original audience was, of course, his sister and her coterie. The seventeenth century, however, saw Sidney's romance appeal to a wider and increasingly less aristocratic audience, for whom such lessons in interpretation would have had fewer resonances with intertextual mannerist play. On the history of *Arcadia*'s reception, see Dennis Kay, ed., *Sir Philip Sidney: An Anthology of Modern Criticism*, esp. 3-41.

CHAPTER 2
Borrowed Authority: Appropriating "Italian Histories"

1. Puttenham, *Arte of Poesie*, 19; Nashe, "Preface to *Menaphon*" 3:313.
2. Puttenham, *Arte of Poesie*, 74.
3. Greenblatt, *Renaissance Self-Fashioning*, 9. New historicism has, of course, been subject to considerable interrogation, even while it continues to illuminate literary texts. See, for example, Edward Pechter's conclusion that placing "the text back into history (or, better, histories: our histories, its histories) is clearly a valuable project. Maybe it is the only project. In any case it is far too important to be left to the new historicists" ("The New Historicism and Its Discontents: Politicizing Renaissance Drama," 302). For other critiques, see Jean E. Howard's "The New Historicism in Renaissance Studies" (3–33) and H. Aram Veeser's collection, *The New Historicism*, particularly its afterward by Stanley Fish.
4. F. O. Matthiessen, *Translation: An Elizabethan Art*, 3. See also H. A. Mason, *Humanism and Poetry in the Early Tudor Period*; C. H. Conley, *The First English Translators of the Classics*; and the discussion of sixteenth-century theorists in Susan Bassnett-McGuire, *Translation Studies*, 53–58. It is important to stress the existence of female translators in sixteenth-century England. Tina Krontiris, in "Breaking Barriers of Genre and Gender: Margaret Tyler's Translation of *The Mirrour of Knighthood*," asserts that Elizabethan English culture accepted women as translators since translation "called for a relatively passive role and indirectly reinforced the idea of an author as patriarch" (23). For additional discussion of Tyler, see Lucas, *Writing for Women*, 11. See also Elizabeth McCutcheon's comments on the popularity of translation among educated women in "The Learned Woman in Tudor England: Margaret More Roper" (449–80), and Phoebe Sheavyn, *The Literary Profession in the Elizabethan Age*, 159.

As important as translation was to the period, sixteenth-century England produced no codified theory of translation. As Bassnett-McGuire observes, Chapman's repetition of the principles of Etienne Dolet's *La manière de bien traduire d'une langue en aultre* (1540) in the dedication to his translation of the first seven books of Homer's *Iliad* comes closest to such a statement in English (54). See also Thomas Steiner's "Precursors to Dryden: English and French Theories of Translation in the Seventeenth Century," 50–81. The concept of imitation received more critical attention in the period, but the overlap between imitation and translation was not clear. As Marjorie Donker and George M. Muldrow explain, translation prior to the sixteenth century was closely tied to the analysis of texts. Only in the sixteenth century did translations arise whose primary purpose was "to enrich from foreign stores a developing vernacular literature" (*Dictionary of Literary-Rhetorical Conventions in the English Renaissance*, 128).

5. For a discussion of Riche's attitudes toward fashion, see John Edward Price's "'Because I would followe the Fashion': Rich's *Farewell to the Military Profession* and Shakespeare's *Twelfth Night*."
6. J. M. Cohen, *English Translators and Translations*, 13. Italian texts were frequently translated into English from French translations. One notable example of this procedure is Geoffray Fenton's *Historie of Guicciardin*, based on the 1568 French translation by Chomeday. See Sidney Alexander, "On Translating from Renaissance Italian," 23.

7. Salzman, *Prose Fiction*, 7; Conley, *First English Translators*, 2; Mason, *Humanism and Poetry*, 24; Cohen, *Translators and Translations*, 9; R. A. Knox, *On English Translation*, 18; Burton Raffel, *The Forked Tongue: A Study of the Translation Process*, 12. These critics suggest the difficulty involved in distinguishing imitation from translation during the period. For a detailed analysis of Renaissance concepts of imitation, see Jacqueline Miller's *Poetic License* and Thomas Greene's *The Light in Troy: Imitation and Discovery in Renaissance Poetry*.

An issue related to the sense of translation described here is the "discovered manuscript" topos. When a text's narrator claims merely to be a translator or editor of a manuscript that has fallen into his or her hands (as in Gascoigne's *Master F. J.* or Lodge's *A Margarite of America*), a similar kind of looseness is found. "Editors" of such texts are able to distance themselves from the alleged intentions of a work in a fashion similar to that of translators who view their goal as cultural diffusion and the enrichment of their national literature. In both cases, the "author" of the text becomes merely a ruse for the "editor's" words.

8. Salzman, *Prose Fiction*, 9-10, 17; Margolies, *Novel and Society*, 26; Kinney, *Humanist Poetics*, 205. Walter R. Davis's emphasis on thematic development keeps his focus away from the translation process in the works he discusses.

9. Diane Shklanka, ed. *A Critical Edition of George Whetstone's 1582 An Heptameron of Civill Discourses*, 330, 125. In *Italian Social Customs of the Sixteenth Century and Their Influence on the Literature of Europe*, Thomas F. Crane describes Whetstone's *Heptameron* as "the most elaborate original production of [its] kind in English literature, and ... deserving of rescue from the oblivion into which it has fallen" (520). On the other hand, in *The Renaissance in England* Hyder E. Rollins and Herschel Baker call Whetstone "perhaps the least interesting of all the uninteresting writers ... in the lean years between Tottel's *Miscellany* and *The Shepherd's Calendar*" (312).

10. Angell Daye, trans., *Daphnis and Chloe*, 74. For additional discussion of this aspect of Daye's *Daphnis and Chloe*, see Howard C. Cole's *Quest of Inquirie*, 484-86. For Philisides's eclogue, see Sidney, *The Old Arcadia*, 222.

11. Walter Benjamin, "The Task of the Translator," 73, 78; Mason, *Humanism and Poetry*, 24. There are similarities between my assessment of Benjamin's attitudes toward translation and Bakhtin's discussion of hybrid novelistic genres in *The Dialogic Imagination* (41-83). Such translation theories as Benjamin's or those of the writers anthologized in Joseph F. Graham's *Difference in Translation* vary considerably from those held by working translators. See Lewis Galantiere, ed., *The World of Translation: Papers Delivered at the Conference on Literary Translation;* Burton Raffel, *The Forked Tongue;* or Donald Frame's "Pleasures and Problems of Translation." Frame, much more modest about translation's status than Benjamin, claims that translation "belongs far below good literary creation, and below good literary analysis" even though it "demands much of the same sensitivity" as those acts (70).

12. This analytical method was suggested by Leah S. Marcus's opening chapter of *Puzzling Shakespeare: Local Reading and Its Discontents*.

13. Xenophon's *Cyropaedia* was typically considered by sixteenth-century English culture as a fictional history to be classified with Greek romances. See, for example, Sidney's *Defence of Poetry*, which cites Heliodorus's *Æthiopica* and Xenophon's text as evidence that poetry is not limited to works in verse (27). Its

genre still troubles contemporary scholarship. Thomas Hägg observes that its "amount of pure fiction is too great to allow it to be called history or biography, in the modern sense" (*The Novel in Antiquity,* 113). Barker's translation of Xenophon has been edited by James Tatum as *The School of Cyrus: William Barker's 1567 Translation of Xenophon's* Cyropaedeia (*The Education of Cyrus*).

14. On the nature of Elizabethan title pages, see Margery Corbett and Ronald Lightblown, *The Comely Frontispiece: The Emblematic Title-Page in England, 1550–1660* (1–47), although their focus is primarily on title pages for which it is possible to assert a high degree of authorial involvement. Theodore Lowe De Vinne's *The Practice of Typography: A Treatise on Title-Pages* establishes even more clearly that title pages were generally the printer's, not the author's, concern. For use of "social energy," see Stephen Greenblatt's *Shakespearean Negotiations: The Circulation of Social Energy in Renaissance England,* esp. 6–7.

15. The very visual nature of Riche's title page urges readers to view it as emblematic; however, the fact that its design was also used by the printer, John Kingston, for Riche's *The Straunge and Wonderful Aduentures of Don Simonides* (1581) and *The Aduentures of Brusanus* (1592) argues against reading its images in this way. (See Beecher, *Barnabe Riche,* 106.) The emphasis of Riche's motto on the economic pun inherent in his name removes the *Farewell* from the realm of courtly discourse and stresses Riche's desire to authorize himself within the context of the marketplace.

16. Harold Ogden White comments briefly on the nature of Riche's translations, stating that the freedom with which Riche handles Continental texts in the *Farewell* makes his versions of the stories "his stories, original in the classical and Elizabethan sense, and therefore he does not call them translations, but tales which had 'neuer been ... published in printe'" (*Plagiarism and Imitation During the English Renaissance,* 110–11). White does not consider the role of L. B. in this process.

17. For a more complete discussion of Bryskett's probable relationship to Riche and the *Farewell,* see Riche, *Farewell,* xxii–xxxvi. See also Thomas E. Wright's *Lodowick Bryskett: A Discourse of Civill Life,* especially his discussion of Bryskett's life, which interestingly makes no mention of Barnabe Riche or the *Farewell.*

18. Riche, *Farewell,* xxvi–xxxii. Lucas, however, notes that the translated narratives do not include any direct addresses to Riche's readers, a technique common to most of the remaining stories of the *Farewell* (*Writing for Women,* 106–7).

19. For specific comparisons between Riche's adaptations and the Italian text, see Giraldi Cinthio's *Hecatommithi,* Decade VI, novel 3; Decade II, novel 6; and, Decade III, novel 5. For Cranfill's assessment of the quality of the novellas Riche translated, see Riche, *Farewell,* xxii, xxxv.

20. Northrop Frye, *The Anatomy of Criticism: Four Essays,* 44. Possible qualifications to this conclusion occur in the first and seventh texts in the *Farewell.* In "Sappho," the restoration of husband and wife to each other and to their social rank is at least as important to the narrative's conclusion as the prosperous marriages their children contract. In this instance, the members of the older generation who prosper are, in effect, symbolically transferred to the younger generation. "Aramanthus borne a Leper" involves not only the romantic relationship of a young couple, but also the rekindling of the love between an older couple who, with the younger generation, live "in quietness, with many long

and happie daies" (179). Nonetheless, the social order has been reconfigured through the marriage between the daughter of the Turk and the European Aramanthus.

21. Walter R. Davis isolates a different kind of tie among the three translated texts. Without developing why these novellas are included in Riche's work, he notes that the three stories present "hypotheses" that test ideals: Gonsales "explicitly puts a set of inherited precepts to the test," "Lucilla's exhibition of the Idea of chastity in her person changes Don Hercules from a lecher to benefactor, and in the fourth tale the ideal love of Fineo and Fiamma has a similar effect on the king of Tunis" (*Idea and Act*, 43-44). Lucas argues that the translated tales all depict "in different ways how the virtues of chastity and loyalty in women restore relationships and, indeed, save lives" (*Writing for Women*, 106).

22. Lucas argues that female readers of Riche's *Farewell* are "not invited to enter into a relationship" with the heroines of the translated novellas because the solutions they find to "male violence and authority" are not political, but personal (*Writing for Women*, 107).

23. A phrase taken from Frances Keene's "For the Embattled Reader" (27-32), an essay on translation's role under oppressive governments.

CHAPTER 3
Constructing Voice, Subverting Narrative

1. Margolies, *Novel and Society*, 44. Lennard J. Davis, in *Factual Fictions*, makes a similar point but sees these subversive possibilities as much more prominent in later fiction and does not discuss sixteenth- or seventeenth-century English texts within this context. Richard Helgerson's *The Elizabethan Prodigals*, in contrast, emphasizes the ways in which Gascoigne, Lyly, Greene, Lodge, and Sidney exploited perceptions of themselves in the creation of their fiction. As will become clear, especially in my discussion of Greene's cony-catching pamphlets, I will argue that there is an important distinction to be made between presentation of an authorial self and the construction of a narrative voice.

2. Barthes, "Introduction," 287. See Bakhtin's discussion in *The Dialogic Imagination* of the ways in which the novelist incorporates various genres into the production of an internally dialogized, heteroglot text operating on the borders of the literary. The production of such a text requires obscuring of the codes that produced it. Especially crucial to my argument is Tzvetan Todorov's insistence that in *The Poetics of Prose* "no narrative is natural; a choice and a construction will always preside over its appearance; narrative is a discourse, not a series of events. . . . [A]ll narratives are figurative" (55).

3. Elizabethan criminal literature, as is well known, is intimately involved with the development of prose fiction in English. See, for example, discussions of Greene's pamphlets in Walter R. Davis, Lennard J. Davis (*Factual Fictions*), Kinney, Salzman, and Schlauch (*Antecedents*). A second form of early fiction, the jest book, is also significant in this context. Gradually, the individual jests began to emphasize one character, or a group of characters, that helped create lengthier texts. On the relation of jest books to the development of fiction, see (in addition

to the relevant sections of the texts cited above) Avril S. O'Brien's *"Dobsons Drie Bobbes:* A Significant Contribution to the Development of Prose Fiction."

4. William C. Dowling, *Jameson, Althusser, Marx: An Introduction to* The Political Unconscious, 96-97; Fredric Jameson, *The Political Unconscious: Narrative as a Socially Symbolic Act*; Wallace Martin, *Recent Theories of Narrative,* 187.

5. Gerard Genette, *Narrative Discourse: An Essay in Method,* 229. In opposition to a definition of narrative based on the presence of a narrative voice, Barthes argues: "There is no doubt that the apersonal is the traditional mode of narrative, language having developed a whole tense system peculiar to narrative (based on the aorist), designed to wipe out the present of the speaker. As Benveniste puts it: 'In narrative, no one speaks'" (283). The impersonality cited here is itself a fiction aimed at producing the disinauguration necessary in order to accomplish fiction's role as an ideological critique.

6. See Kittay and Godzich, *Emergence of Prose,* 130-31.

7. Walter Benjamin, "The Storyteller: Reflections on the Works of Nikolai Leskov," 69-82.

8. Wayne C. Booth. *The Rhetoric of Fiction,* 75, 177. Booth's entire argument on the nature of authorial voice (169-266) bears on this discussion, although I am not certain that these terms fully describe the experience of the texts I discuss, texts for which the basic cultural experience of the reader might vary wildly. Nonetheless, Booth's terms stress an important point: a written text creates both its writer and its readers. Elizabethan novelistic prose actively works, through its creation of narrative structures, to transform its writers into "authors" and define the class of its readers in opposition to cultural and historical concerns.

9. For a discussion of Harmon's *A Caveat for Common Cursitors,* see, for instance, A. V. Judges's commentary on Harmon's text, *The Elizabethan Underworld* (495); Salzman, *Prose Fiction,* 205; and, Sandra Clark, *The Elizabethan Pamphleteer: Popular Moralistic Pamphlets, 1580-1640,* 43-44.

10. Stephen Greenblatt's brief discussion of Harmon's *Caveat* in "Invisible Bullets" calls attention to "the spice of betrayal" that he feels is caused by Harmon's disclosure of information he swore to keep secret (*Shakespearean Negotiations,* 50). While Greenblatt sees more of this "spice" in the text than I do, he also stresses the text's emphasis on seeming to present "accurate observation."

11. The pamphlets to be discussed are: *A Notable Discouery of Coosnage, The Second Part of Conny-catching, The Thirde and Last Parte of Conny-catching, A Disputation betweene a Hee Conny-catcher and a Shee Conny-catcher, The Blacke Bookes Messenger, The Defence of Conny-catching.* All references to these texts will be to *The Life and Complete Works in Prose and Verse of Robert Greene, M.A.,* edited by Alexander B. Grosart. Clark discusses Greene's pamphlets in relation to earlier rogue literature. Walter R. Davis, however, classifies the pamphlets as part of the "literature of fact" (*Idea and Act,* 183). Helgerson finds in the pamphlets qualities of what Ian Watt terms "realism of presentation" while simultaneously recognizing that much of the contents of these works are "catchpenny collections of jestbook tales" (*Elizabethan Prodigals,* 8, 104). See also *Three Elizabethan Pamphlets,* 15-16, and Salzman, *Prose Fiction,* 206. Kinney, in *Humanist Poetics,* also emphasizes the error of treating the pamphlets as fact. He asserts that Greene turns his readers "into his conies, tricked into buying and studying his exposés convinced they are factual rather than fiction" (335). I would shift Kinney's emphasis in two ways. First, the object

of "study" in these pamphlets is not the criminal world but rather the nature of Robert Greene himself. Secondly, the similarities between Greene's conycatching pamphlets and the jest book and rogue literature traditions lessens the reader's tendency to accept the pamphlets as factual accounts that deserve "study." A comment should be made here about the terms "fact" and "fiction," which cannot help but resonate with the overtones they gather from Lennard J. Davis's *Factual Fictions*. I am drawing on his sense of these terms and his work describing the interaction of these two categories. "Fact" and "fiction," he reminds us, are not "two distinct and unimpeachable categories" but instead ends of a continuum (9).

12. This discussion somewhat simplifies the structure of *A Disputation*. The debate between Nan and Lawrence is followed by the first-person narrative of the "Conuersion of an English Courtizan" (10:237-76). Greene's narrative voice provides a brief interlude between the two main sections of the work, and it also supplies a concluding jest about the deception of a sick man by his caregiver, and his subsequent revenge. A further, but unrelated, point of interest should be made here about *A Disputation*. Although Linda Woodbridge's *Women and the English Renaissance: Literature and the Nature of Womankind, 1540-1620* does not include it in the discussion of the Renaissance debate about women, it deserves to be considered seriously within that context as well. It places its female character in the classic position of having to defend women's nature, only to have "her" ultimately prove that women are by far more evil than men.

13. Robert Greene, *Complete Works* 10:40. Margolies has provided the most conclusive evidence for Greene's authorship of *The Defence*. His research shows that the preface to the reader in one edition of *The Defence* (STC 5655) simply repeats a preface from *A Notable Discouery*, but it changes its identified author from Robert Greene to Cuthbert Cunny-catcher (109-10). For arguments against Greene's authorship, see I. A. Shapiro, "An Unsuspecting Earlier Edition of *The Defence of Conny-catching*"; David Parker's rebuttal, "Robert Greene and the *Defence of Conny-catching*"; and A. F. Allison, *Robert Greene, 1558-1592: A Bibliographical Catalogue of the Early Editions in England (to 1640)*.

14. This identification is suggested by Grosart in Robert Greene, *Complete Works* 11:303.

15. The narrative structure of *The Thirde and Last Parte of Conny-catching* deserves special mention. In its preface Greene represents himself as being at a dinner party with a gentleman privy to court information, which he supplies to Greene. The main body of the pamphlet is said to derive from this gentleman's notes. Yet, its narrative voice seems indistinguishable from that of the other pamphlets allegedly written in Greene's own voice, and the narrator refers to himself and his observations of events in the first person, leaving the reader uncertain as to the identity of the "I" of the text. By creating this doubt, the reader's attention is further centered on the figure of Greene as narrator.

16. For analyses of the pamphlets that see them progressing away from a social agenda, see, for example, Hibbard, *Three Elizabethan Pamphlets*, 23; Walter R. Davis, *Idea and Act*, 185-86. Reid Barbour has recently argued that Greene attempts to achieve an "aggressive" mode of narrative control "that regulates the society in which his readers live" (*Deciphering Elizabethan Fiction*, 45).

17. See Ann Rosalind Jones's "Inside the Outsider: Nashe's *Unfortunate Traveller* and Bakhtin's Polyphonic Novel" for a discussion of the discontinuities in Nashe's work in relation to Bakhtin's theories of Menippean genres and the polyphonic novel.

18. An examination of the bibliographies on Riche compiled in James L. Harner's *English Renaissance Prose Fiction, 1500–1600: An Annotated Bibliography of Criticism* shows the popularity of "Apolonius and Silla" as a topic of research. Eight of thirty-nine entries in Harner's 1978 edition specifically discuss this story, as do five of the eighteen entries in the 1985 edition and four of the nine listings in his 1992 bibliography. Given the number of Riche's publications, the amount of energy devoted to "Apolonius and Silla" is certainly noteworthy.

19. In "Phylotus and Emelia," the final text in the collection, Riche explores literal cross-dressing but rejects the pronomial cross-dressing he indulges in here.

20. Price's essay, "'Because I would followe the Fashion,'" discusses these epistles within a different context (to establish connections between Riche's *Farewell* and *Twelfth Night* in regard to clothing styles), and he finds within them a less contradictory nature than will be described in the following argument.

21. In this sense, it seems to build on the argument Riche presented in his *Allarme to England* (1578), which includes, as its title page explains, "a short discourse conteyning the decay of warlike discipline, conuenient to be perused by Gentlemen, such as are desirous by seruice, to seeke . . . the preseruation of the countrey."

22. In "Barnaby Rich and King James," T. M. Cranfill quotes the following statement about James's reaction to the third edition of the *Farewell*, written in 1595 by George Nicholson, servant to the English ambassador to Scotland, as partial explanation for Riche's substituting "the Turke" for King James in the 1606 edition: "In the conclusion of a booke in England called Rich his farewell printed by V.S. for Tho. Adams at the signe of the white lyon in Paules Churchyard 1594 such matter is noted as the *King* is not well pleased therat; so as one grief comes in thend of another, it wold please the *King* some thinck that some order were taken therewith. The *King* saies litle but thinkes more" (67).

John Lyly also aligns clothing and literary fashions in *Euphues*'s preface to its gentlemen readers: "In my mynde Printers and Taylors are bound chiefely to pray for Gentlemen, the one hath so many fantasies to print, the other such diuers fashions to make, that the pressing yron of the one is neuer out of the fyre, nor the printing presse of the other any tyme lyeth still. But a fashion is but of dayes wearing, and a booke but an howres reading" (*Complete Works of John Lyly* 1:182).

CHAPTER 4
Gender, Empowerment, and the Construction of Character

1. Susan Dwyer Amussen, *An Ordered Society: Gender and Class in Early Modern England*, 187.

2. Among Amussen and others, see also Woodbridge on changes in sixteenth-century English culture that altered women's roles.

3. In a related argument on the role of women in defining economic relations in early modern England, Lisa Jardine, in *Still Harping on Daughters*, suggests that Elizabethan sumptuary laws reflect women's centrality to sixteenth- and seventeenth-century economics and their value in male society (141-68).

4. On Deloney's exaggeration to serve class ends, see, among others, Salzman, who describes Deloney's protagonists as "highly idealized figures" who represent a good deal of "wish-fulfilment" (*Prose Fiction*, 103). Salzman is justifiably critical, however, of viewing Deloney as a middle-class novelist, and he describes accurately the difficulties and potential for anachronism involved in identifying Deloney with the "middle class" (102). On Riche's relationship to his female readers, see Lucas's conclusion that "the sympathy Rich has is for his women characters, not his women readers" (*Writing for Women*, 112).

5. Elaine Showalter, "Towards a Feminist Poetics," 170. Margaret Tyler's translation is discussed briefly by Hull and more extensively by Tina Krontiris. Study of early prose fiction by women, especially *Urania*, has recently become more vigorous. See, for example, Mary Ellen Lamb's exploration of *Urania* in *Gender and Authorship in the Sidney Circle* and Naomi J. Miller's "'Not much to be marked': Narrative of the Woman's Part in Lady Mary Wroth's *Urania*."

6. Elaine Showalter, "Feminist Criticism in the Wilderness," 199-200.

7. Paul Jorgensen, "Barnaby Rich: Soldierly Suitor and Honest Critic of Women," 183. It could certainly be argued that in his preface to soldiers Riche is employing a variety of "realism" akin to Watt's "formal realism." The distinctions between Riche's strategy and that of later writers of prose fiction centers on the conscious way in which Riche's preface avoids creating a seamless fictional world and prevents his readers from placing his narrator within the world he describes. The distinctions between factuality and fiction, to draw upon Lennard J. Davis, are not fully differentiated within Riche's text, and so appeals to realism and factuality can be clearly seen as fictional.

8. In his preface to soldiers, Riche presents an anecdote mocking an effeminately dressed man that emphasizes this implication. Cross-dressing, especially male adoption of female fashion, was generally seen by early modern English culture as a mark of individual and cultural depravity since it obscured differences between the sexes and distorted their "natural" hierarchy.

9. Woodbridge does consider an interlude from Riche's *Brusanus* to be part of the formal controversy, as well as his *Faultes, Faults, and Nothing Else But Faults* (1606) and *The Excellencie of Good Women* (1613). On the role Queen Elizabeth played in literary representations of the period's misogyny, see Louis A. Montrose, "*A Midsummer Night's Dream* and the Shaping Fantasies of Elizabethan Culture: Gender, Power, Form," 65-87; and, Leah S. Marcus, "Shakespeare's Comic Heroines, Elizabeth I, and the Political Uses of Androgyny," 135-53.

10. See Hull, *Chaste*, 77.

11. See Kelly-Gadol, "Did Women Have a Renaissance?"

12. Lodge, *Rosalynde*, 255.

13. Thomas Deloney, *The Gentle Craft, Part I*, in *The Novels of Thomas Deloney*, 143; references to Deloney's work will be to this edition by page number.

14. For a different treatment of the character of Long Meg, see *The Life and Pranks of Long Meg of Westminster*, in which, as Charles C. Mish explains, she

"loves to fight but is saved from being a virago by her unexpected but winning wifely submission after she is married" (81).

15. In addition to Woodbridge's study, see also Carroll Camden, *The Elizabethan Woman;* Ruth Kelso, *The Doctrine for the Lady of the Renaissance;* Sara J. Eaton, "Presentations of Women in the English Popular Press"; and, Constance Jordan, *Renaissance Feminism: Literary Texts and Political Models.*

16. Sidney's *The Old Arcadia* also employs the notion of the Ovidian character metamorphosed by the effects of love. Philoclea's wish that Cleophila "might become a young transformed Caeneus" (98), who had been transformed into a man by Neptune, is granted almost immediately by Cleophila's revelation that she is, in fact, Pyrocles.

17. In "Sappho," however, there are perceived differences of status and economics that are not present here; that text also contains more explicit laws governing parental control of children's marriages.

18. On similarities between this play and Riche's "Twoo Brethren," see Cranfill's comments in Riche, *Farewell,* xliii-l.

19. This is an example of the *caritas romana* motif—more typical in paintings than literature—of the daughter, Pero, who saves her imprisoned father, Cimon, from starvation by breast-feeding him. Riche alters the tradition significantly, however, by eliminating the generational difference and geneological similarity by transforming the nursing woman into the prisoner's wife. See Axel Steensberg, "*Caritas Romana,* or the Story of the Imprisoned Cimon and his Self-Sacrificing Daughter," 9-36. Lucas cites this passage as evidence that "woman's life-giving qualities are celebrated, and Isabel's devotion to her husband vividly demonstrated" by the tale (*Writing for Women,* 107).

CHAPTER 5
Authorizing Landscapes: The Power of Place

1. E. M. Forster, *Aspects of the Novel,* 21, 22. In *The English Novel: From the Earliest Days to the Death of Joseph Conrad,* Ford Madox Ford issues a similar dismissal, claiming that *when* Elizabethan fiction is of interest, it is only because of "the verbal juggleries of the author. I have read *Euphues* once at least right through and have looked into it several times—but I have not the least idea what it is about" (63).

2. Frederick R. Karl, *The Eighteenth-Century English Novel,* 13, 14. In *Before Novels* J. Paul Hunter presents a much less dogmatic view of the novel's characteristic traits. Nonetheless, he emphasizes "contemporaneity" and "familiarity" as common to the novel (23), features that, I would argue, blend easily into notions of realism. Ian Watt asserts that formal realism relies on "the premise, or primary convention, that the novel is a full and authentic report of human experience, and is therefore under an obligation to satisfy its reader with such details of the story as the individuality of the actors concerned, the particulars of the times and places of their actions, details which are presented through a more largely referential use of language than is common in other literary forms" (*Rise of the Novel,* 32).

3. Samuel Johnson, *The History of Rasselas, Prince of Abyssinia*, 90. For Karl's discussion of the novel's possibilities as a subversive genre, see *The Eighteenth-Century Novel*, 3-54.

4. Todorov, *Poetics of Prose*, 67.

5. Raymond Williams, *The Country and the City*, 42-43. I do not intend to suggest that specific detailed descriptions do not occur elsewhere in the novelistic discourse of the period. See, for instance, Nashe's description of the banqueting house in Rome in *The Unfortunate Traveller* or the treatment of Jack of Newbury's parlor in Deloney's novel. Still, such descriptions are notable because of their infrequency.

6. Nicholas Breton, *The Miseries of Mavillia*, in *The Collected Verse and Prose of Nicholas Breton*, 35-51; all references to Breton's text will be to this edition. For criticism of *The Miseries of Mavillia* that discusses its realism, see Salzman, *Prose Fiction*, 87-88, 367, 377; Walter R. Davis, *Idea and Act*, 200, 216; and, especially, Schlauch, *Antecedents*, 216ff. Despite his praise for the narrative style of *Mavillia*, Salzman dismisses Breton's work as "an interesting curiosity" (88).

7. Here, as elsewhere in this chapter, I am strongly influenced by Raymond Williams's discussions of the pastoral in *The City and the Country*, William Empson's *Some Versions of Pastoral*, and Lennard J. Davis's discussion of novelistic settings in *Resisting Novels: Ideology and Fiction*.

8. Lennard J. Davis, *Resisting Novels*, 84.

9. The kind of distinction being made between the language-based law of Genoa and the tradition-based law of Tunis is analogous to the tension Keith Wrightson discusses between "the order demanded by the law and the problems of maintaining neighborly relationships in the village" present in late-sixteenth-century rural England (*English Society*, 158).

10. Edward W. Said, *Orientalism*, 38-39.

11. Again, notice that the sea transmits the letters but provides no immediate means for the lovers' escape from Tunis: according to Genoese law, language must precede action.

12. This conclusion further supports the analysis of the narrative that results from positioning translation as the significant Other in relation to which the text defines its artistic authority.

CHAPTER 6
Constructing the Alien, Authorizing the Self

1. Kittay and Godzich, *Emergence of Prose*, 103. For amplification of the notion of collective identity, see Stephen Greenblatt's discussion of Martin Guerre as "the *product* of the relations, material objects, and judgments exposed in [his] case rather than the *producer* of these relations, objects, and judgments" ("Psychoanalysis and Renaissance Culture," 216). Viewed in Greenblatt's terms, Guerre becomes definable only in relation to the village as a whole. Identity becomes an aspect of communal life.

2. It is important to remember that, as Samuel Chew notes, distinctions among Turks, Moors, and Jews during the Elizabethan period were often vague and ill-defined (*The Crescent and the Rose: Islam and England During the Renaissance*,

104). Anthony Munday, in *The Orator* (1596), helps to establish the link between Jews and Turks by referring to "the Turkes, who overkindly doe suffer such vermine [Jews] to dwell amongst them" (qtd. in Bernard Grebanier, *The Truth About Shylock*, 45). On the presence of the Turk in the 1606 edition of the *Farewell*, see Cranfill, "Barnaby Rich and King James," 71.

3. For more recent scholarship on the literary relationship between the East and Renaissance England, see Eldred D. Jones, *The Elizabethan Image of Africa;* Leslie A. Fiedler, *The Stranger in Shakespeare;* Elliott H. Tokson, *The Popular Image of the Black Man in Renaissance Drama;* and Jack D'Amico, *The Moor in English Renaissance Drama*.

4. Chew, *Crescent*, 491; Eldred D. Jones, *Image of Africa*, 20.

5. The prayer, entitled "The Prayer in this Sermon made for the Church, and all the states thereof," follows John Foxe's *A Sermon of Christ Crucified, preached at Paules Crosse the Friday before Easter, commonly called Goodfryday* (*The English Sermons of John Foxe*, sigs. T2-T3). I have explored the implications of this prayer for understanding attitudes toward the East in other early modern English texts in "Liminal Geography: *Pericles* and the Politics of Place."

6. Geoffray Fenton, *The History of Guicciardin*, 179. The relative faithfulness of Fenton's translation becomes apparent if his text is compared with a twentieth-century translation, such as *The History of Italy*, edited and translated by Sidney Alexander. See Alexander's discussion of Fenton's translation in *The History of Italy* (xxvii) and his "On Translating from Renaissance Italian" on the difficulties of translating Guicciardini's text. On Fenton's elaborations on Guicciardini's history, see Rudolph B. Gottfried, *Geoffrey Fenton's Historie of Guicciardin*, 15, 24.

7. Fenton, *Guicciardin*, sig. A5v.

8. Thomas Newton, *A Notable Historie of the Saracens*, unpaginated dedication.

9. William Painter, *The Palace of Pleasure* 3:395; future references to Painter's work will be to this edition by volume and page.

10. For discussion of Munday's text, see Paul A. Scanlon's "Munday's *Zelauto:* Form and Function." See also Jack Stillinger's commentary in Anthony Munday, *Zelauto;* all references to *Zelauto* will be by page number to this edition.

11. These acts of religious piety differ from English acts of Protestant or Catholic martyrdom in that internal political and religious struggles have been erased in Munday's Persia: political authority and religious authority are incontrovertably joined in the soldan. A secret faction of Christians exists, but it neither has nor seeks any political power. The soldan's decision to execute Christians is harsh, but it meets no political opposition.

12. William Kittle, *Edward de Vere, 17th Earl of Oxford, and Shakespeare*, 47-49. While Persia and Turkey are distinct geographic locations, it is important to remember their easy conflation in much early modern English thought, which permits them to be freely linked in our analysis of the uses to which writers of Elizabethan novelistic discourse put the East, imagined in its broadest sense.

13. Thomas Nashe, *The Unfortunate Traveller*, in *The Complete Works of Thomas Nashe* 2:202; future references to Nashe's text will be to this edition.

14. Kinney, *Humanist Poetics*, 355.

15. Ibid., 344.

16. Chew, *Crescent*, 101n.

17. Fenton, *Guicciardin*, 814.

18. A similar mass conversion occurs at the end of Book One of Lady Mary Wroth's *Urania*. In that instance, however, the King of Cyprus leads all his people in a true conversion (204).

CONCLUSION
Novelistic Discourse and the Problem of Realism

1. Jonathan Culler, "Poetics of the Novel," 193, 238.
2. See, for instance, Todorov's "The Typology of Detective Fiction" (42-52) or Lucas's comparison between contemporary and Renaissance romances (*Writing for Women*, 18-26).

Bibliography

Addison, James Clyde, Jr., ed. *An Old-Spelling Critical Edition of Thomas Lodge's A Margarite of America (1596).* Salzburg Studies in English Literature, vol. 96. Salzburg: Institut für Anglistik und Amerikanistik, Universität Salzburg, 1980.

Alexander, Sidney. "On Translating from Renaissance Italian." In *The World of Translation: Papers Delivered at the Conference on Literary Translation, New York, 1970.* Introduction by Lewis Galantiere. New York: P.E.N. American Center, 1971.

———, trans. *The History of Italy,* by Francesco Guicciardini. New York: Macmillan, 1969.

Allison, A. F. *Robert Greene, 1558–1592: A Bibliographical Catalogue of the Early Editions in England (to 1640).* Folkestone, Kent: Dawson, 1975.

Amussen, Susan Dwyer. *An Ordered Society: Gender and Class in Early Modern England.* Oxford: Basil Blackwell, 1988.

Baker, Ernest A. *The History of the English Novel.* Vol. 2. 1936. Reprint. New York: Barnes and Noble, 1950.

Bakhtin, M. M. *The Dialogic Imagination.* Edited by Michael Holmquist. Translated by Caryl Emerson and Michael Holmquist. Austin: University of Texas Press, 1981.

Baldwin, William. *Beware the Cat: The First English Novel.* Edited by William Ringler and Michael Flachman. San Marino, Calif.: Huntington Library, 1988.

Barbour, Reid. *Deciphering Elizabethan Fiction.* Newark: University of Delaware Press, 1993.

Barthes, Roland. "Introduction to the Structural Analysis of Narratives." In *A Barthes Reader,* edited by Susan Sontag. New York: Hill and Wang, 1982.

Bassnett-McGuire, Susan. *Translation Studies.* New York: Routledge, 1980.

Beecher, Donald, ed. *Barnabe Riche His Farewell to Military Profession.* Publications of the Barnabe Riche Society, vol. 1. Ottawa: Dovehouse Editions, 1992.

Benjamin, Walter. "The Storyteller: Reflections on the Works of Nikolai Leskov." In *Illuminations*, edited by Hannah Arendt. Translated by Harry Cohn. New York: Schocken Books, 1969.

———. "The Task of the Translator." In *Illuminations*, edited by Hannah Arendt. Translated by Harry Cohn. New York: Schocken, 1969.

Booth, Wayne C. *The Rhetoric of Fiction*. 2d ed. Chicago: University of Chicago Press, 1983.

Breton, Nicholas. *The Miseries of Mavillia*. In vol. 2 of *The Collected Verse and Prose of Nicholas Breton*, edited by Alexander B. Grosart. Chertsey Worthies' Library. Edinburgh: Edinburgh University Press, 1879.

Camden, Carroll. *The Elizabethan Woman*. Rev. ed. Mamaroneck, N.Y.: Paul P. Appel, 1976.

Chew, Samuel. *The Crescent and the Rose: Islam and England During the Renaissance*. 1937. Reprint. New York: Octagon, 1965.

Clark, Sandra. *The Elizabethan Pamphleteer: Popular Moralistic Pamphlets, 1580-1640*. London: Athlone Press, 1983.

Cohen, J. M. *English Translators and Translations*. London: Longmans, Green and Co., 1962.

Cole, Howard C. *A Quest of Inquirie*. Indianapolis: Pegasus, 1973.

Conley, C. H. *The First English Translators of the Classics*. 1927. Reprint. Port Washington, N.Y.: Kennikat Press, 1967.

Corbett, Margery, and Ronald Lightbown. *The Comely Frontispiece: The Emblematic Title-Page in England, 1550-1660*. London: Routledge and Kegan Paul, 1979.

Craigie, James. "*Philotus:* A Late Middle Scots Comedy." *Scottish Literary Journal* 6, 1 (1979): 19-23.

Crane, Thomas F. *Italian Social Customs of the Sixteenth Century and Their Influence on the Literature of Europe*. New Haven: Yale University Press, 1920.

Cranfill, T. M. "Barnaby Rich and King James." *ELH* 16 (March 1949): 65-75.

———. "Barnaby Rich's 'Sappho' and *The Weakest Goeth to the Wall*." *University of Texas Studies in English* 25 (1945-46): 142-71.

Cranfill, T. M., and Dorothy Bruce. *Barnaby Rich: A Short Biography*. Austin: University of Texas Press, 1953.

Cressy, David. "Educational Opportunity in Tudor and Stuart England." *History of Education Quarterly* 16 (Fall 1976): 301-20.

Culler, Jonathan. "Poetics of the Novel." *Structuralist Poetics: Structuralism, Linguistics, and the Study of Literature*. Ithaca: Cornell University Press, 1975.

D'Amico, Jack. *The Moor in English Renaissance Drama*. Tampa: University of South Florida Press, 1991.

Davis, Lennard J. *Factual Fictions: The Origins of the English Novel*. New York: Columbia University Press, 1983.

———. *Resisting Novels: Ideology and Fiction*. New York: Methuen, 1987.

Davis, Walter R. *Idea and Act in Elizabethan Fiction*. Princeton: Princeton University Press, 1963.

Daye, Angell. *Daphnis and Chloe*. 1587. London: Elston Press, 1904.

De Vinne, Theodore Lowe. *The Practice of Typography: A Treatise on Title-Pages*. 1901. Reprint. New York: Haskell House Publishers, 1972.

Deloney, Thomas. *The Novels of Thomas Deloney*. Edited by Merritt E. Lawlis. 1961. Reprint. Westport, Conn.: Greenwood Press, 1978.

Donker, Marjorie, and George M. Muldrow, eds. *Dictionary of Literary-Rhetorical Conventions of the English Renaissance*. Westport, Conn.: Greenwood Press, 1982.

Dowling, William C. *Jameson, Althusser, Marx: An Introduction to* The Political Unconscious. Ithaca: Cornell University Press, 1984.

Dubrow, Heather. "A Mirror for Complaints: Shakespeare's *Lucrece* and the Generic Tradition." In *Renaissance Genres: Essays on Theory, History, and Interpretation*, edited by Barbara Kiefer Lewalski. Cambridge: Harvard University Press, 1986.

Eaton, Sara J. "Presentations of Women in the English Popular Press." In *Ambiguous Realities: Women in the Middle Ages and the Renaissance*, edited by Carole Levin and Jeanie Watson. Detroit: Wayne State University Press, 1987.

Eisenstein, Elizabeth L. *The Printing Press as an Agent of Change: Communications and Cultural Transformations in Early-Modern Europe*. 2 vols. New York: Cambridge University Press, 1979.

Elyot, Thomas. *The Boke Named the Governour*. Edited by S. E. Lehmberg. New York: Dutton, 1963.

Empson, William. *Some Versions of Pastoral*. New York: New Directions, 1974.

Fenton, Geoffray. *The Historie of Guicciardin*. 1579. 3d ed. London: Richard Field, 1618.

Fiedler, Leslie A. *The Stranger in Shakespeare*. Frogmore: Paladin, 1974.

Fish, Stanley. "Interpreting the *Variorum*." In *Is There a Text in This Class?* Cambridge: Harvard University Press, 1980.

Ford, Ford Madox. *The English Novel: From the Earliest Days to the Death of Joseph Conrad*. 1930. Reprint. Manchester: Carcanet Press, 1983.

Forster, E. M. *Aspects of the Novel*. New York: Harcourt, 1927.

Fowler, Alastair. "The Life and Death of Literary Forms." In *New Directions in Literary History*, edited by Ralph Cohen. Baltimore: Johns Hopkins University Press, 1974.

Foxe, John. *The English Sermons of John Foxe*. Introduction by Warren W. Wooden. Delmar, N.Y.: Scholars' Facsimiles and Reprints, 1978.

Frame, Donald. "Pleasures and Problems of Translation." In *The Craft of Translation*, edited by John Biguenet and Rainer Schulte. Chicago: University of Chicago Press, 1989.

Frye, Northrop. *The Anatomy of Criticism: Four Essays*. Princeton: Princeton University Press, 1957.

Galantiere, Lewis, ed. *The World of Translation: Papers Delivered at the Conference on Literary Translation, New York, 1970*. New York: P.E.N. American Center, 1971.

Garke, Esther. *The Use of Songs in Elizabethan Prose Fiction*. Bern: Francke Verlag, 1972.

Gascoigne, George. "Certayne Notes of Instruction." In *Elizabethan Critical Essays*. 2 vols. Edited by G. Gregory Smith. Oxford: Clarendon, 1904.

———. *A Discourse of the Adventures Passed by Master F.J.* In *A Hundreth Sundrie Flowres*, edited by C. T. Prouty. 1942. Reprint. Columbia: University of Missouri Press, 1970.

Genette, Gerard. *Narrative Discourse: An Essay in Method*. Translated by Jane E. Lewin. Ithaca: Cornell University Press, 1980.

Giraldi Cinthio, Giovanni Battista. *Gli Hecatommithi*. In vol. 2 of *Raccolta di novelliere italiani*. Florence: Borghi, 1833.

Gottfried, Rudolph B. "Geoffray Fenton's *Historie of Guicciardin.*" Indiana University Publications, Humanities Series, no. 3. Bloomington: Indiana University Press, 1940.
Graham, Joseph F., ed. *Difference in Translation*. Ithaca: Cornell University Press, 1985.
Grebanier, Bernard. *The Truth About Shylock*. New York: Random House, 1962.
Greenblatt, Stephen. "Psychoanalysis and Renaissance Culture." In *Literary Theory/Renaissance Texts*, edited by Patricia Parker and David Quint. Baltimore: Johns Hopkins University Press, 1986.
———. *Renaissance Self-Fashioning: From More to Shakespeare*. Chicago: University of Chicago Press, 1980.
———. *Shakespearean Negotiations: The Circulation of Social Energy in Renaissance England*. Berkeley: University of California Press, 1988.
Greene, Robert. *The Life and Complete Works in Prose and Verse of Robert Greene*, M.A. 15 vols. Edited by Alexander B. Grosart. London: The Huth Library, 1881-83.
Greene, Thomas. *Light in Troy: Imitation and Discovery in Renaissance Poetry*. New Haven: Yale University Press, 1982.
Hägg, Thomas. *The Novel in Antiquity*. Berkeley: University of California Press, 1983.
Hall, Anne Drury. *Ceremony and Civility in English Renaissance Prose*. University Park: Pennsylvania State University Press, 1991.
Harington, Sir John. *A Preface or rather a Briefe Apologie of Poetrie*. In *Elizabethan Critical Essays*. 2 vols. Edited by G. Gregory Smith. Oxford: Clarendon, 1904.
Harmon, Thomas. *A Caveat for Common Cursitors*. In *Rogues, Vagabonds, and Sturdy Beggars: A New Gallery of Tudor and Early Stuart Rogue Literature*, edited by Arthur F. Kinney. Amherst: University of Massachusetts Press, 1990.
Harner, James L. *English Renaissance Prose Fiction, 1500-1600: An Annotated Bibliography of Criticism*. 2d ed. Boston: G. K. Hall, 1985.
———. *English Renaissance Prose Fiction, 1500-1660: An Annotated Bibliography of Criticism (1984-1990)*. New York: G. K. Hall, 1992.
Harrison, G. B., ed. *Menaphon by Robert Greene and A Margarite of America by Thomas Lodge*. Oxford: Basil Blackwell, 1927.
Harvey, Gabriel. *Foure Letters*. In *Elizabethan Critical Essays*. 2 vols. Edited by G. Gregory Smith. Oxford: Clarendon, 1904.
Helgerson, Richard. *The Elizabethan Prodigals*. Berkeley: University of California Press, 1976.
Hibbard, G. R., ed. *Three Elizabethan Pamphlets*. 1951. Reprint. Freeport, N.Y.: Books for Libraries, 1969.
Hill, Christopher. *Reformation to Industrial Revolution*. The Pelican Economic History of Britain, vol. 2. Baltimore: Penguin, 1967.
Howard, Jean. "The New Historicism in Renaissance Studies." In *Renaissance Historicisms: Selections from English Literary Renaissance*, edited by Arthur F. Kinney and Dan S. Collins. Amherst: University of Massachusetts Press, 1987.
Hull, Suzanne. *Chaste, Silent and Obedient: English Books for Women, 1475-1600*. San Marino, Calif.: Huntington Library, 1982.

Hunter, J. Paul. *Before Novels: The Cultural Contexts of Eighteenth-Century English Fiction.* New York: W. W. Norton, 1990.

———. "'News, and New Things': Contemporaneity and the Early English Novel." *Critical Inquiry* 14 (Spring 1988): 493–515.

Imbrie, Ann. "Defining Nonfiction Genres." In *Renaissance Genres: Essays on Theory, History, and Interpretation,* edited by Barbara Kiefer Lewalski. Cambridge: Harvard University Press, 1986.

Jameson, Fredric. *The Political Unconscious: Narrative as a Socially Symbolic Act.* Ithaca: Cornell University Press, 1981.

Jardine, Lisa. *Still Harping on Daughters: Women and Drama in the Age of Shakespeare.* Totowa, N.J.: Barnes and Noble, 1983.

Johnson, Samuel. *The History of Rasselas, Prince of Abyssinia.* In *Selected Poetry and Prose,* edited by Frank Brady and W. K. Wimsatt. Berkeley: University of California Press, 1977.

Jones, Ann Rosalind. "Inside the Outsider: Nashe's *Unfortunate Traveller* and Bakhtin's Polyphonic Novel." *ELH* 50 (Spring 1983): 61–82.

Jones, Eldred D. *The Elizabethan Image of Africa.* Washington, D.C.: Folger Shakespeare Library, 1971.

Jordan, Constance. *Renaissance Feminism: Literary Texts and Political Models.* Ithaca: Cornell University Press, 1990.

Jorgensen, Paul. "Barnaby Rich: Soldierly Suitor and Honest Critic of Women." *Shakespeare Quarterly* 7 (Spring 1956): 183–88.

Judges, A. V. *The Elizabethan Underworld.* 1930. Reprint. London: Routledge and Kegan Paul, 1965.

Jusserand, J. J. *The English Novel in the Time of Shakespeare.* Translated by Elizabeth Lee. 1890. Reprint. New York: AMS Press, 1965.

Karl, Frederick R. *The Eighteenth-Century English Novel.* New York: Noonday, 1974.

Kay, Dennis, ed. *Sir Philip Sidney: An Anthology of Modern Criticism.* Oxford: Oxford University Press, 1987.

Keene, Frances. "For the Embattled Reader." In *The World of Translation: Papers Delivered at the Conference on Literary Translation, New York, 1970.* Introduction by Lewis Galantiere. New York: P.E.N. American Center, 1971.

Kelly-Gadol, Joan. "Did Women Have a Renaissance?" In *Becoming Visible: Women in European History,* edited by Renate Bridenthal and Claudia Koonz. Boston: Houghton Mifflin, 1977.

Kelso, Ruth. *The Doctrine for the Lady of the Renaissance.* Urbana: University of Illinois Press, 1956.

King, Margaret L. *Women of the Renaissance.* Women in Culture and Society, edited by Catharine R. Stimpson. Chicago: University of Chicago Press, 1991.

Kinney, Arthur F. *Humanist Poetics: Thought, Rhetoric, and Fiction in Sixteenth-Century England.* Amherst: University of Massachusetts Press, 1986.

Kittay, Jeffrey, and Wlad Godzich. *The Emergence of Prose: An Essay in Prosaics.* Minneapolis: University of Minnesota Press, 1987.

Kittle, William. *Edward de Vere, 17th Earl of Oxford, and Shakespeare.* Baltimore: Monumental Printing, 1942.

Knox, R. A. *On English Translation.* Oxford: Clarendon, 1957.

Krontiris, Tina. "Breaking Barriers of Genre and Gender: Margaret Tyler's Translation of *The Mirrour of Knighthood.*" *ELR* 18 (Winter 1988): 19–38.

Lamb, Mary Ellen. "The Countess of Pembroke and the Art of Dying." In *Women in the Middle Ages and the Renaissance: Literary and Historical Perspectives.* Syracuse: Syracuse University Press, 1986.

———. *Gender and Authorship in the Sidney Circle.* Madison: University of Wisconsin Press, 1990.

Lievsay, John Leon. "A Word About Barnaby Rich." *Journal of English and Germanic Philology* 55, 3 (1956): 381–92.

Linton, Joan Pong. "*Jack of Newbery* and Drake in California: Domestic and Colonial Narratives of English Cloth and Manhood." *ELH* 59 (Spring 1992): 23–51.

Lodge, Thomas. *Margarite of America.* In Menaphon *by Robert Greene and* A Margarite of America *by Thomas Lodge,* edited by G. B. Harrison. Oxford: Basil Blackwell, 1927.

———. *Rosalynde.* In vol. 2 of *Narrative and Dramatic Sources of Shakespeare,* edited by Geoffrey Bullough. New York: Columbia University Press, 1958.

Lucas, Caroline. *Writing for Women: The Example of Woman as Reader of Elizabethan Romance.* Philadelphia: Open University Press, 1989.

Lukács, Georg. *The Theory of the Novel.* Translated by Anna Bostock. Cambridge: MIT Press, 1971.

Lyly, John. *The Complete Works of John Lyly.* 3 vols. Edited by R. Warwick Bond. 1902. Reprint. Oxford: Clarendon Press, 1973.

McCutcheon, Elizabeth. "The Learned Woman in Tudor England." In *Women Writers of the Renaissance and Reformation,* edited by Katharina Wilson. Athens: University of Georgia Press, 1987.

McKeon, Michael. *The Origins of the English Novel, 1600–1740.* Baltimore: Johns Hopkins University Press, 1987.

Marcus, Leah S. *Puzzling Shakespeare: Local Reading and Its Discontents.* Berkeley: University of California Press, 1988.

———. "Shakespeare's Comic Heroines, Elizabeth I, and the Political Uses of Androgyny." In *Women in the Middle Ages and the Renaissance: Literary and Historical Perspectives,* edited by Mary Beth Rose. Syracuse: Syracuse University Press, 1986.

Margolies, David. *Novel and Society in Elizabethan England.* London: Croom Helm, 1985.

Martin, Wallace. *Recent Theories of Narrative.* Ithaca: Cornell University Press, 1986.

Mason, H. A. *Humanism and Poetry in the Early Tudor Period.* London: Routledge and Kegan Paul, 1959.

Matthiessen, F. O. *Translation: An Elizabethan Art.* Cambridge: Harvard University Press, 1931.

Miller, Jacqueline T. *Poetic License: Authority and Authorship in Medieval and Renaissance Contexts.* Oxford: Oxford University Press, 1986.

Miller, Naomi J. "'Not much to be marked': Narrative of the Woman's Part in Lady Mary Wroth's *Urania.*" *Studies in English Literature* 29 (Winter 1989): 121–37.

Miner, Earl. "Some Issues of Literary 'Species or Distinct Kind.'" In *Renaissance Genres: Essays on Theory, History, and Interpretation,* edited by Barbara Kiefer Lewalski. Cambridge: Harvard University Press, 1986.

Mirollo, James V. *Mannerism and Renaissance Poetry: Concept, Mode, Inner Design.* New Haven: Yale University Press, 1984.

Mish, Charles C., ed. *Short Fiction of the Seventeenth Century.* New York: New York University Press, 1963.

Montrose, Louis A. "*A Midsummer Night's Dream* and the Shaping Fantasies of Elizabethan Culture: Gender, Power, Form." In *Rewriting the Renaissance: The Discourses of Sexual Difference,* edited by Margaret W. Ferguson, Maureen Quilligan, and Nancy Vickers. Chicago: University of Chicago Press, 1986.

Mueller, Janel. *The Native Tongue and the Word: Developments in English Prose Style, 1380–1580.* Chicago: University of Chicago Press, 1984.

Munday, Anthony. *Zelauto.* Edited by Jack Stillinger. Carbondale: Southern Illinois University Press, 1969.

Nash, Ralph, ed. and trans. *Arcadia and Piscatorial Eclogues,* by Jacopo Sannazaro. Detroit: Wayne State University Press, 1966.

Nashe, Thomas. *The Works of Thomas Nashe.* 5 vols. Edited by Ronald B. McKerrow. Corrections and supplementary notes by F. P. Wilson. Oxford: Basil Blackwell, 1958.

Nelson, William. *Fact or Fiction: The Dilemma of the Renaissance Storyteller.* Cambridge: Harvard University Press, 1973.

―――. "From 'Listen Lordings' to 'Dear Reader.'" *University of Toronto Quarterly* 46 (Winter 1976-77): 110-24.

Newton, Thomas. *A Notable Historie of the Saracens.* 1575. The English Experience, no. 863. Norwood, N.J.: Walter J. Johnson, 1977.

O'Brien, Avril S. "*Dobsons Drie Bobbes:* A Significant Contribution to the Development of Prose Fiction." *Studies in English Literature* 12 (Winter 1972): 55-70.

Ong, Walter J. *Orality and Literacy: The Technologizing of the Word.* New York: Methuen, 1982.

Painter, William. *The Palace of Pleasure.* 3 vols. Edited by Joseph Jacobs. London: David Nutt, 1890.

Parker, David. "Robert Greene and 'The Defence of Conny-catching.'" *Notes and Queries* n.s. 21, no. 3 (1974): 87-89.

Pechter, Edward. "The New Historicism and Its Discontents: Politicizing Renaissance Drama." *PMLA* 102 (May 1987): 292-303.

Philmus, M. R. Rohr. "Gascoigne's Fable of the Artist as a Young Man." *Journal of English and Germanic Philology* 73, 1 (1974): 13-31.

Price, John Edward. "'Because I would followe the Fashion': Rich's *Farewell to the* [sic] *Military Profession* and Shakespeare's *Twelfth Night.*" *Iowa State Journal of Research* 62, 3 (1988): 397-406.

Prouty, C. T. *George Gascoigne: Elizabethan Courtier, Soldier, and Poet.* New York: Columbia University Press, 1942.

―――, ed. *George Gascoigne's* A Hundreth Sundrie Flowres. 1942. Reprint. Columbia: University of Missouri Press, 1970.

Puttenham, George. *The Arte of English Poesie.* Kent English Reprints Series. Introduction by Baxter Hathaway. Kent, Ohio: The Kent State University Press, 1970.

Raffel, Burton. *The Forked Tongue: A Study of the Translation Process.* The Hague: Mouton, 1971.

Relihan, Constance C. "Liminal Geography: *Pericles* and the Politics of Place." *Philological Quarterly* 71 (Summer 1992): 281-99.
Rice, Warner G. "The Moroccan Episode in Thomas Heywood's *The Fair Maid of the West*." *Philological Quarterly* 9 (January 1930): 131-40.
Riche, Barnabe. *The Aduentures of Brusanus Prince of Hungaria*. London, 1592.
———. *Allarme to England, foreshewing what perilles are procured, where the people liue without regarde of Martiall lawe*. London, 1578.
———. *Rich's Farewell to Militarie Profession (1581)*. Edited by T. M. Cranfill. Austin: University of Texas Press, 1959.
———. *The Straunge and Wonderful Aduentures of Don Simonides*. 2 vols. London, 1581, 1584.
Rollins, Hyder E., and Herschel Baker. *The Renaissance in England*. Lexington, Mass.: D. C. Heath, 1954.
Rowe, George E., Jr. "Interpretation, Sixteenth-Century Readers, and George Gascoigne's 'The Adventures of Master F. J.'" *ELH* 48 (Summer 1981): 271-89.
Said, Edward W. *Orientalism*. New York: Vintage, 1978.
Salzman, Paul. *English Prose Fiction 1558-1700: A Critical History*. Oxford: Clarendon, 1985.
Sannazaro, Jacopo. *Arcadia and Piscatorial Eclogues*. Translated and edited by Ralph Nash. Detroit: Wayne State University Press, 1966.
Scanlon, Paul A. "Munday's *Zelauto:* Form and Function." *Cahiers Élisabéthains* 18 (October 1980): 11-15.
Schlauch, Margaret. *Antecedents of the English Novel, 1400-1600: From Chaucer to Deloney*. London: Oxford, 1963.
———. "English Short Fiction in the 15th and 16th Centuries." *Studies in Short Fiction* 3 (Summer 1966): 393-434.
Shapiro, I. A. "An Unsuspecting Earlier Edition of *The Defence of Conny-catching*." *The Library* 5th ser., 18, 1 (1963): 88-112.
Sheavyn, Phoebe. *The Literary Profession in the Elizabethan Age*. 2d ed. Revised by J. W. Saunders. New York: Barnes and Noble, 1967
Shklanka, Diana, ed. *A Critical Edition of George Whetstone's 1582 An Heptameron of Civill Discourses*. The Renaissance Imagination, vol. 35, edited by Stephen Orgel. New York: Garland, 1987.
Showalter, Elaine. "Feminist Criticism in the Wilderness." *Critical Inquiry* 8 (Winter 1981): 179-205.
———. "Towards a Feminist Poetics." In *Women Writing and Writing About Women*, edited by Mary Jacobus. 1979. Reprinted in *Contemporary Literary Criticism*, edited by Robert Con Davis. New York: Longman, 1986.
Sidney, Sir Philip. *The Countess of Pembroke's Arcadia*. Edited by Maurice Evans. New York: Penguin, 1979.
———. *A Defence of Poetry*. Ed. Jan Van Dorsten. Oxford: Oxford University Press, 1966.
———. *The Old Arcadia*. Edited by Katherine Duncan-Jones. Oxford: Oxford University Press, 1985.
Smith, Barbara Herrnstein. "Poetry as Fiction." In *New Directions in Literary History*, edited by Ralph Cohen. Baltimore: Johns Hopkins University Press, 1974.

Smith, G. Gregory, ed. *Elizabethan Critical Essays*. 2 vols. Oxford: Clarendon, 1904.
Spender, Dale. *Mothers of the Novel: 100 Good Women Writers Before Jane Austen*. New York: Pandora, 1986.
Spingarn, Joel E. *Critical Essays of the Seventeenth Century.* 3 vols. 1908-9. Reprint. Bloomington: Indiana University Press, 1957.
Spufford, Margaret. *Small Books and Pleasant Histories: Popular Fiction and Its Readership in Seventeenth-Century England*. London: Methuen, 1981.
Starnes, D. T. "Barnabe Riche's 'Sappho Duke of Mantona': A Study in Elizabethan Story-Making." *Studies in Philology* 30 (July 1933): 445-72.
Steadman, John M. *Redefining a Period Style: "Renaissance," "Mannerist" and "Baroque" in Literature*. Pittsburgh: Duquesne University Press, 1990.
Steensburg, Axel. "*Caritas Romana*, or the Story of the Imprisoned Cimon and his Self-Sacrificing Daughter." In *Caritas Romana: The Concept of Culture*. Translated by Alexander Fenton. Copenhagen: National Museum of Denmark, 1976.
Steiner, Thomas. "Precursors to Dryden: English and French Theories of Translation in the Seventeenth Century." *Comparative Literature Studies* 7 (March 1970): 50-81.
Stevenson, Laura Caroline. *Praise and Paradox: Merchants and Craftsmen in Elizabethan Popular Literature*. Cambridge: Cambridge University Press, 1984.
Stone, Lawrence. *The Crisis of the Aristocracy*. Oxford: Oxford University Press, 1965.
Tatum, James, ed. *The School of Cyrus: William Barker's 1567 Translation of Xenophon's Cyropaedeia (The Education of Cyrus)*. The Renaissance Imagination, vol. 37, edited by Stephen Orgel. New York: Garland, 1987.
Todorov, Tzvetan. *The Poetics of Prose*. Translated by Richard Howard. Ithaca: Cornell University Press, 1977.
Tokson, Elliot H. *The Popular Image of the Black Man in Renaissance Drama*. Boston: G. K. Hall, 1982.
Veeser, H. Aram, ed. *The New Historicism*. New York: Routledge. 1989.
Vickers, Nancy. "'The blazon of sweet beauty's best: Shakespeare's *Lucrece*." In *Shakespeare and the Question of Theory*, edited by Patricia Parker and Geoffrey Hartman. New York: Methuen, 1985.
Watt, Ian. *The Rise of the Novel*. Berkeley: University of California Press, 1957.
Webbe, William. *A Discourse of Englishe Poetrie*. In *Elizabethan Critical Essays*. 2 vols. Edited by G. Gregory Smith. Oxford: Clarendon, 1904.
Whigham, Frank. *Ambition and Privilege: The Social Tropes of Elizabethan Courtesy Theory*. Berkeley: University of California Press, 1984.
White, Harold Ogden. *Plagiarism and Imitation During the English Renaissance*. Harvard Studies in English, vol. 12. Cambridge: Harvard University Press, 1935.
Williams, Raymond. *The Country and the City*. New York: Oxford University Press, 1973.
Wilson, Katharina, ed. *Women Writers of the Renaissance and Reformation*. Athens: University of Georgia Press, 1987.
Woodbridge, Linda. *Women and the English Renaissance: Literature and the Nature of Womankind, 1540-1620*. Urbana: University of Illinois Press, 1984.

Woolf, Virginia. "*The Countess of Pembroke's Arcadia.*" In *The Second Common Reader.* 1932. Reprint. New York: Harcourt, Brace and World, 1960.
Wright, Louis B. *Middle-Class Culture in Elizabethan England.* Chapel Hill: University of North Carolina Press, 1935.
———. "The Reading of Renaissance English Women." *Studies in Philology* 28 (October 1931): 149–56.
Wright, Thomas E., ed. *Lodowick Bryskett: A Discourse of Civill Life.* Northridge, Calif.: San Fernando Valley State College, 1970.
Wrightson, Keith. *English Society, 1580–1680.* New Brunswick: Rutgers University Press, 1982.
Wroth, Lady Mary. *The Countess of Montgomery's Urania, Book 1.* In *An Anthology of Seventeenth-Century Fiction,* edited by Paul Salzman. New York: Oxford University Press, 1991.

Index

Adventures of Brusanus Prince of Hungaria, The (Riche), 7, 149n.12, 157n.9
Adventures of Master F. J., The (Gascoigne), 2, 35, 58, 60, 102, 148n.7; poetry in, 18, 19, 21-23, 24, 30, 31, 151n.7
Allarme to England (Riche), 156n.21
Amussen, Susan, 78-79
"Apolonius and Silla" (Riche), 70-72, 75, 76, 121, 137-38
Apuleius, 60
"Aramanthus borne a Leper" (Riche), 95, 96-97, 121, 124, 127, 131-36, 137
Arcadia (Sannazaro), 17, 32
Arcadia (Sidney), 2, 15, 17, 25, 119, 141, 149n.21; continuation of, 80; poetry in, 19, 21, 24, 32, 39; Virginia Woolf on, 21
Ardener, Edwin, 81
Arte of Englishe Poesie, The (Puttenham), 9, 33-34, 36
As You Like It (Shakespeare), 50, 86
Ascham, Roger, 15, 37

Bacon, Sir Francis, 9
Bakhtin, M. M., 3-4, 56, 57, 100, 153n.2
Baldwin, William, 3

Bandello, Matteo, 38
Barker, William, 42, 44, 46
Barthes, Roland, 55-56, 154n.5
Benjamin, Walter, 39-40, 59
Bennett, H. S., 2
Beyazid (Bajazeth) II, Ottoman Sultan, 121, 123
Blacke Bookes Messenger, The (Greene), 63, 65-67
Boccaccio, Giovanni, 9; *De Claris Mulieribus*, 92; *Decameron*, 14, 38, 60, 104
Booth, Wayne C., 60, 154n.8
Breton, Nicholas, *The Miseries of Mavillia*, 13, 14, 79, 102-8, 109, 117-18, 159n.6; narrative voice of, 102-3
Bryskett, Lodowick, 48-49, 52-53

Caritas Romana topos, 158n.19
Castiglione, Baldesar, 15
Caveat for Common Cursitors, A (Harmon) 2, 56, 61-62, 68, 70, 74, 75, 101
Cavendish, Margaret, 80
Cebik, L. B., 57
Chaucer, Geoffrey, 14, 92
Chew, Samuel, 121-22, 123
Churchyard, Thomas, 24
Cohen, J. M., 37

Colonization of Eastern cultures, 121–23
Complaint genre, 22–23
Continental novellas, 35, 40–44, 45, 46–48
Cony-catching pamphlets, 56–57, 61–70, 74, 75–76
Corbett, Margery, and Ronald Lightblown, 46
Countess of Montgomery's Urania, The (Wroth), 80, 161n.18
Cranfill, T. M., 25, 48–49; and Dorothy Bruce, 6–7
Cressy, David, 13, 146n.18
Criminal pamphlets, 56–57, 61–70, 74, 75–76; description within, 101
Cross-dressing, 86, 89–94, 157n.8
Culler, Jonathan, 140–42
Cyropaedeia (Xenophon; trans. W. Barker), 42, 44, 46, 151n.13

Daphnis and Chloe (Longus; trans. A. Daye), 39, 131
Davis, Lennard J., 3, 108, 153n.1, 154n.11, 157n.7
Davis, Walter R., 8, 124, 153n.21
Daye, Angell, 39
Decameron (Boccaccio), 14, 38, 60, 104
Defence of Conny-catching, The (Greene), 63–65, 66, 69, 155n.13
Defence of Poetry, A (Sidney), 9, 151n.13
Deloney, Thomas, 2, 10, 13, 21, 58, 79, 95, 97; E. M. Forster on, 100; *The Gentle Craft*, 2, 80, 86, 87–89, 98; *Jack of Newbury*, 2, 6, 13, 18, 20, 24, 31, 149n.12; *Thomas of Reading*, 14, 79, 142
de Navarre, Marguerite, *The Heptameron*, 38, 60
De Vinne, Theodore Lowe, 152n.14
Descriptive techniques, 99–102; in Breton's *Miseries of Mavillia*, 102–8, 117–18; pre-novelistic, 108; in Riche's *Farewell*, 108–18
Detective fiction, 142
Diana, La (Montemayor), 17

"Discovered manuscript" topos, 151n.7
Disinauguration of narrative voice, 70; and Breton's *Miseries of Mavillia*, 103; defined by Barthes, 55–56
Disputation betweene a Hee Conny-catcher and a Shee Conny-catcher, A (Greene), 63, 65, 66–67, 155n.12
Donker, Marjorie, and George M. Muldrow, 150n.4
Dowling, William, 57

Eastern cultures, 5; in Munday's *Zelauto*, 120, 127–29, 138; in Nashe's *The Unfortunate Traveller*, 120, 129–30, 139; as Other, 111, 119–25, 126; in Painter's *Palace of Pleasure*, 120, 125–27, 138; in Riche's *Farewell*, 120, 130–39
Education: of Elizabethan children, 13–14; of Elizabethan girls, 13–14, 146nn.19–20
Elizabeth I, of England, 74, 84, 122, 128, 141
Elizabethan novelistic discourse: audience defined, 11, 12–15, 59, 60, 82–84, 119–20, 136, 146n.15; authors' economic position, 10, 11–12, 60; descriptive techniques employed, 99 118; Eastern cultures, 119–39; female characters, 77–98; foreign sources, 33–54; generalized landscapes, 102, 104–8; Judaism, 125, 129–30; lack of realism, 99–102; marketplace's role in the development of, 10–11, 60; and narrative voice, 91–133; poetry, 17–32
Euphues and His England (Lyly), 15
Eupheus: The Anatomy of Wit (Lyly), 2, 6, 102, 148n.5, 156n.22
Excellencie of Good Women, The (Riche), 157n.9

Faerie Queene, The (Spenser), 14
Faultes, Faults and Nothing Else But Faultes (Riche), 157n.9

INDEX

Female characters within Elizabethan novelistic discourse, 77–98
Fenton, Geoffray: *Certain Tragicall Discourses*, 38; *The History of Guicciardin*, 123–24, 125, 133, 150n.6
"Fineo and Fiamma" (Riche), 6, 49, 50, 52, 102, 108–18, 136–37
Ford, Ford Madox, 158n.1
Formal realism, 3, 100, 102, 158n.2
Forster, E. M., 99–100
Fowler, Alastair, 3
Foxe, John, 122–23, 128
Frame, Donald, 151n.11
Fraser, Antonia, 14
Frye, Northrop, 50

Garke, Esther, 149n.13
Gascoigne, George, 10, 21, 141; *The Adventures of Master F. J.*, 2, 35, 58, 60, 102, 148n.7; "Certayne Notes of Instruction," 9–10; poetry in *The Adventures of Master F. J.*, 18, 19, 21–23, 24, 30, 31, 151n.7
Genette, Gerard, 58
Gentle Craft, The (Deloney), 2, 80, 86, 87–89, 98
Giraldi Cinthio, Giovanni Battista, 6, 35, 38, 48, 49–50, 51, 53, 108–9; and Riche's "Nicander and Lucilla," 27, 32
Golden Ass, The (Apuleius), 60
"Gonsales and his Wife Agatha" (Riche), 49, 51–52, 53, 95, 97
Greenblatt, Stephen, 15, 35, 44, 77, 94, 98, 99, 159n.1
Greene, Robert, 141, 145n.13, 153n.1; *The Blacke Bookes Messenger*, 63, 65–66, 66–67; cony-catching pamphlets, 2, 56, 61, 62–70, 72, 74, 141, 154n.11; *The Defence of Conny-catching*, 63–65, 66, 69, 155n.13; *A Disputation betweene a Hee Conny-catcher and a Shee Conny-catcher*, 63, 65, 66–67, 155n.12; *A Notable Discovery of Coosnage*, 63, 66, 68, 155n.13; *Pandosto*, 79, 102; *The Second Part of Conny-catching*, 63, 66; *The Thirde and Last Parte of Conny-catching*, 63, 155n.15
Grosart, Alexander B., 64
Guicciardini, Francesco, 123–24, 125

Hägg, Thomas, 152n.13
Hall, Anne Drury, 145n.12
Harington, Sir John, 10
Harmon, Thomas, *A Caveat for Common Cursitors*, 2, 56, 61–62, 68, 70, 74, 75, 101
Harvey, Gabriel, 10
Hecatommithi (Giraldi Cinthio) 6, 35, 38, 48, 49–50, 51, 53, 108–9; and Riche's "Nicander and Lucilla," 27, 32
Helgerson, Richard, 147n.4, 153n.1, 154n.11
Heliodorus, 9, 151n.13
Heptameron, The (de Navarre), 38, 60
Heptameron of Ciuill Discourses, The (Whetstone), 38–39, 42, 44, 46, 53, 151n.9
Hibbard, G. R., 62
Hill, Christopher, 13
Hull, Suzanne, 8, 14, 146n.20
Hunter, J. Paul, 158n.2

Imbrie, Ann, 145n.12
Italian humanism, 59

Jack of Newbury, 2, 6, 13, 18, 20, 24, 31, 149n.12
James I of England, James VI of Scotland, 74, 156n.22
Jameson, Fredric, 57–58
Jardine, Lisa, 147n.20, 157n.3
Jestbooks, 8, 153n.3
Johnson, Samuel, 100–101, 118
Jorgensen, Paul, 82, 83
Judaism: identification with Islam in Elizabethan culture, 120, 159n.2; in Nashe's *The Unfortunate Traveller*, 120, 129–30, 139

Karl, Frederick, 100–102, 108, 136
Kelly-Gadol, Joan, 85, 146n.20

King, Margaret L., 146n.19
Kinney, Arthur F., 25, 38, 130, 154n.11
Kittay, Jeffrey, and Wlad Godzich, 119, 144n.2
Kittle, William, 128
Knox, R. A., 37
Krontiris, Tina, 150n.4

Landscapes described in Elizabethan novelistic discourse, 102, 104-8, 108-18
Lepanto, Battle of, 122
Lievsay, John Leon, 7
Lightblown, Ronald, and Margery Corbett, 46
Literacy, 2; and Elizabethan educational practices, 12-15; rates during Elizabethan period, 2, 13, 146n.18
Lodge, Thomas, 10, 21, 141, 149n.21, 153n.1; *A Margarite of America*, 15, 18-20, 24, 31, 60, 119, 147n.4, 151n.7; *Rosalynde*, 71, 79, 80, 85-87, 97, 98, 141
Long Meg of Westminster, 147n.14
Longus, *Daphnis and Chloe*, 39, 131
Lucas, Caroline, 149n.20, 152n.18, 153n.21, 153n.22, 157n.4, 158n.19
Lukàcs, Georg, 4
Lyly, John, 58, 70, 141; *Euphues: The Anatomy of Wit*, 2, 6, 102, 148n.5, 156n.22; *Euphues and His England*, 15

McKeon, Michael, 3
Malory, Sir Thomas, 17, 24
Mannerism, 19, 149n.21
Margarite of America, A (Lodge), 15, 18-20, 24, 31, 60, 119, 147n.4, 151n.7
Margolies, David, 6, 11-12, 38, 55, 56, 136, 155n.13
Martin, Wallace, 57, 64
Mason, H. A., 36, 37, 40
Matthiesen, F. O., 36
Measure for Measure (Shakespeare), 38

Mercantile classes: growth of in Elizabethan England, 59, 79, 98; readers of Elizabethan novelistic discourse, 136
Merry Wives of Windsor (Shakespeare), 96
Metamorphoses (Ovid), 92
Midsummer Night's Dream, A (Shakespeare), 50
Military life: Elizabethan devaluation of, 7, 131-32; in Riche's "To the noble Souldiours," 72, 73-74, 81, 82-85
Miller, E. H., 2
Miller, Jacqueline, 9
Miner, Earl, 23, 144n.4
Mirror for Magistrates, The, 22-23, 24
Miseries of Mavillia, The (Breton), 13, 14, 79, 102-8, 109, 117-18, 159n.6; narrative voice of, 102-3
Montemayor, Jorge de, 17
Moors, representation of in Elizabethan culture, 120, 122, 125, 126-27, 136
Morte Darthur (Malory), 17, 24
Mulcaster, Richard, 14
Muldrow, George M., and Marjorie Donker, 150n.4
Munday, Anthony: *The Orator*, 160n.2; *Zelauto*, 39, 120, 127-29, 130, 138, 160n.11

Narrative voice, 4, 32, 38, 70; in Breton's *The Miseries of Mavillia*, 102-3; construction of in Elizabethan novelistic discourse, 55-76; in Greene's cony-catching pamphlets, 61, 62-70, 75-76; in Harmon's *Caveat for Common Cursitors*, 61-62, 70, 75; in Riche's *Farewell*, 70-76, 82
Nashe, Thomas, 2, 141; Preface to *Menaphon*, 10, 33-34, 37; *The Unfortunate Traveller*, 2, 15, 18, 36, 110, 139, 142; *The Unfortunate Traveller*, narrative voice of, 58, 59; *The Unfortunate Traveller*,

Nashe, Thomas (*cont.*)
    representation of Judaism in, 120, 125, 129-30
Nelson, William, 17
Newton, Thomas, 125
"Nicander and Lucilla" (Riche), 49, 52, 78, 79, 95-96, 97, 98, 133; poetry in, 18, 24-25, 26-32
Notable Discovery of Coosnage, A (Greene), 63, 66, 68, 155n.13

Old Arcadia, The (Sidney), 15, 58, 71, 158n.16
Ottoman empire, 120-22, 123-24
Overburian character, 61
Ovid, 92

Painter, William, 2, 38; "A Cruell Fact of Soltan Solyman," 120, 125-26, 138; "The Kinge of Marrocco," 120, 126-27, 138; *The Palace of Pleasure*, 2, 4, 42-46, 53, 120, 130
Pamphleteer, 10-11
Pamphlets, 3, 24, 60; as non-literary, 60; status of their authors, 11
Pandosto (Greene), 79, 102
Pechter, Edward, 150n.3
"Phylotus and Emelia" (Riche), 51, 86, 89-95, 97
Poetry, 21, 23, 144n.2; in Deloney's *Jack of Newbury*, 18, 20, 24, 31; in early modern debates on literary forms, 3, 9-10; economics' role in definition of, 23; in Gascoigne's *Adventures of Master F. J.*, 18, 21-22, 23, 24, 31; in Lodge's *A Margarite of America*, 18-20, 24, 31; in prose fiction, 17-24, 31-32, 34; in Riche's "Nicander and Lucilla," 18, 26-31; in Riche's "Sappho Duke of Mantona," 18, 24-26, 31; in Sidney's *Arcadia*, 21, 32
Printing: advent of in Elizabethan England, 58; and translation, 37, 40

Prouty, C. T., 148n.7
Puttenham, George, 9, 33-34, 36

Raffel, Burton, 38
Rape of Lucrece, The (Shakespeare), 22-23, 24, 32
Realism, 3, 141-42; lack of in Elizabethan novelistic discourse, 116; as term used to devalue Elizabethan novelistic discourse, 99-101, 108
Riche, Barnabe, 11-12, 21, 82, 135; biography of, 6-7; *The Adventures of Brusanus Prince of Hungaria*, 7, 149n.12, 157n.9; *Allarme to England*, 156n.21; *The Excellencie of Good Women*, 157n.9; *Faultes, Faults and Nothing Else But Faultes*, 157n.9; *The Straunge and Wonderful Adventures of Don Simonides*, 7, 149n.12, 157n.9. See also *Riche His Farewell to Militarie Profession*
Riche His Farewell to Militarie Profession (Riche), 2, 4, 15, 38, 74-75, 88, 141; "Apolonius and Silla," 70-72, 75, 76, 121, 137-38; "Aramanthus borne a Leper," 95, 96-97, 121, 124, 127, 131-36, 137; Bryskett as translator of portions, 48-49, 52-53; conclusion of, 72, 74-75, 76, 121, 156n.22; critical reception of, 7-8; descriptive techniques in, 108-18; Eastern cultures in, 120, 130-39; Elizabeth I, 84; the female in, 80, 81-85, 86, 88, 89-98; and female readers, 8, 48, 52, 82-85, 94, 98, 153n.22; "Fineo and Fiamma," 6, 49, 50, 52, 102, 108-18, 136-37; "Gonsales and his Wife Agatha," 49, 51-52, 53, 95, 97; narrative voice of, 70-76, 82; "Nicander and Lucilla," 18, 24-32, 49, 52, 78, 79, 95-96, 97, 98, 133; "Phylotus and Emelia," 51, 86, 89-95, 97; poetry in, 18, 25-31; prefaces to, 70, 72-75, 81-85, 132; "Sappho

Duke of Mantona," 6, 8, 18, 24–26, 30–31, 46, 78, 92–93, 95, 97, 121, 132, 137–38; title page of, 42, 46–48; "To the noble Souldiours," 72, 73–74, 81, 82–85, 95; "To the Readers in General," 35, 72, 74, 83; "To the right courteous gentlewomen," 72–73, 82, 94; translated texts in, 42, 46–54, 149n.15, 152n.16; Turks, 120–21, 123, 127, 128, 129, 130–38, 139; "Twoo Brethren," 6, 14, 79, 88, 95–96, 97, 149n.12
Rollins, Hyder E., and Herschel Baker, 151n.10
Romance, 2, 3, 142, 149n.12; conventions, 25, 27, 32, 97; Greek, 6, 109, 147n.4
Rosalynde (Lodge), 71, 79, 80, 85–87, 97, 98, 141

Said, Edward W., 121, 125
Salzman, Paul, 38, 63, 157n.4, 159n.6; on literacy rates, 2, 13
Sannazaro, Jacopo, 17, 32
"Sappho Duke of Mantona" (Riche), 6, 8, 46, 92–93, 121, 132, 137–38; poetry in, 18, 24–26, 30–31; representations of the female in, 78, 95, 97
Scanlon, Paul A., 127
Schlauch, Margaret, 8
Science fiction, 142
Second Part of Conny-Catching, The (Greene), 63, 66
Selim I (Selim the Grim), Ottoman Sultan, 121
Shakespeare, William: *As You Like It*, 50, 86; *Measure for Measure*, 38; *Merry Wives of Windsor*, 96; *A Midsummer Night's Dream*, 50; *The Rape of Lucrece*, 22–23, 24, 32; *Twelfth Night*, 70–71; *A Winter's Tale*, 131
Showalter, Elaine, 80, 81
Sidney, Sir Philip, 10, 48, 153n.1; *Arcadia*, 2, 15, 17, 19, 21, 24–25, 32, 39, 80, 119, 141, 149n.21; *A Defence of Poetry*, 9, 151n.14; *The Old Arcadia*, 15, 58, 71, 158n.16
Smith, Barbara Herrnstein, 149n.11
Song of Roland, The, 120
Spender, Dale, 14
Spenser, Edmund, *The Faerie Queene*, 14
Spufford, Margaret, 12–13, 14
Stevenson, Laura Caroline, 11, 136, 146n.20
Stone, Lawrence, 11, 12, 149n.19; critical response to Stone's work, 145n.15
Straunge and Wonderful Adventures of Don Simonides, The (Riche), 7, 149n.12, 157n.9
Suleiman the Magnificent, Ottoman Sultan, 132

Thirde and Last Parte of Connycatching, The (Greene), 63, 155n.15
Thomas of Reading (Deloney), 14, 79, 142
Title pages, 41–42, 44; of Barker's translation of Xenophon, 42, 44, 46; Corbett and Lightblown on, 46; De Vinne on, 152n.14; of Painter's *Palace of Pleasure*, 42–44, 46; of Riche's *Farewell*, 42, 46–48; of Whetstone's *Heptameron*, 42, 44–46
Todorov, Tzvetan, 56, 101, 153n.2
Translation: to authorize Elizabethan novelistic discourse, 33–40, 150n.4; and the printing press, 37, 40; in Riche's *Farewell*, 42, 46–48, 48–54, 149n.15, 152n.16; theories of, 150n.4, 151n.11
Turks, 74, 122, 125; as antichrists, 132; conversions of in early modern fiction, 161n.18; linked with Jews in Elizabethan culture, 159n.2; linked with Persians in Elizabethan culture, 160n.12; in Riche's *Farewell*, 120–21, 123, 127–39; stereotyped within Elizabethan culture, 120, 121–25
Twelfth Night (Shakespeare), 70–71

"Twoo Brethren" (Riche), 6, 14, 79, 88, 95-96, 97, 149n.12
Tyler, Margaret, 80

Unfortunate Traveller, The (Nashe), 2, 15, 18, 36, 110, 139, 142; narrative voice of, 58, 59; representation of Judaism in, 120, 125, 129-30

Vives, Juan Luis, 15

Watt, Ian, 3, 8, 100, 102, 146n.18, 158n.2
Weamys, Anne, 80
Webbe, William, 10
Whetstone, George, *The Heptameron of Ciuill Discourses,* 38-39, 42, 44, 53, 151n.10
Whigham, Frank, 15
Williams, Raymond, 102
Winter's Tale, A (Shakespeare), 131
Women: as audience for Elizabethan novelistic discourse, 83-84, 146n.20; Elizabethan education of, 13-14, 146n.19, 147.21; as Elizabethan translators, 150n.4; formal controversy over nature of, 84, 155n.12; position within early modern English culture, 80-81; representations of in Deloney's *The Gentle Craft,* 80, 86, 87-89, 97-98; representations of in Lodge's *Rosalynde,* 80, 85-87, 97; representations of in Riche's *Farewell,* 80, 81-85, 86, 88, 89-98; as thematic concern, 5; as threatening Other, 77, 94. See also *Riche His Farewell to Militarie Profession,* and female readers
Woodbridge, Linda, 84
Woolf, Virginia, 21
Wright, Louis B., 11, 14, 145n.15
Wrightson, Keith, 159n.9
Wroth, Lady Mary, 80, 161n.18

Xenophon, 42, 44, 46, 151n.13

Zelauto (Munday), 39, 120, 127-29, 130, 138, 160n.11

FASHIONING AUTHORITY
was composed in 10½-point Baskerville
on a Penta system with CG8600 output
by Berman Electronic Prepress, Inc.;
printed by sheetfed offset
on Glatfelter 60-pound acid-free B-16 stock,
notch case bound into 88-point binder's boards
in Holliston Kingston Natural cloth,
and wrapped with dustjackets printed in two colors
on 70-pound Simpson EverGreen stock
(recycled from 50% waste paper)
by Thomson-Shore, Inc.;
designed by Will Underwood;
and published by
The Kent State University Press
KENT, OHIO 44242